559
Home-Making Hints

...plus scores of recipes and scraps

COLLECTED BY

DR. VIOLA WALDEN

SWORD OF THE LORD PUBLISHERS
P. O. Box 1099, Murfreesboro, Tennessee 37133

ISBN 0-87398-274-6

Printed in the U. S. A.

TABLE OF CONTENTS

HOME-MAKING HINTS:

TIPS for PLEASANT LIVING

1. Don't Hoard Medicine.

Most medicines outlive their usefulness quickly, and some of them become harmful with age. Buy small quantities; hoarding medicine doesn't pay.

2. Dispose of Out-Dated Medicine. . .

and remember to empty bottles down the drain, and rinse thoroughly to safeguard children.

3. Keep a Record of Family Sizes.

Make a card with a complete record of the sizes of the various articles of clothing your family wears. Then when you find a bargain, you will know exact sizes and can take advantage of it.

4. Safety Grip for Bottles.

To provide a safety grip for household bleach and ammonia, stretch two or three rubber bands around the bottle, and it will not slip out of your hands when wet and soapy.

5. Non-Skid Rugs.

Sew a couple of fruit jar rings on the underneath side of small rugs to keep them from slipping.

6. Used Christmas Cards.

Never throw away old Christmas cards. Wrap them up and send to an orphanage, they will provide hours of entertainment for small children. Or cut out some of the beautiful pictures and use for decorations on your Christmas packages.

7. Make Use of Baby Food Jars

to keep snaps, hooks and eyes, paper clips, rubber bands, or thumb tacks handy and in one place on your desk.

8. How to Unstick Stamps.

Postage stamps that have become stuck together can easily be separated by placing them in the refrigerator or freezer for awhile.

9. How Not to Forget Special Occasions.

You will not forget anniversaries and birthdays if, on the first day of every month, you address the cards you plan to mail during the month and arrange them in chronological order. Mark the date when you want to mail in the corner where you paste the postage stamp.

10. Luminous Paint on Pull Cord.

Save bumping into furniture, fumbling in the dark, and hunting for the light by putting luminous paint on the tip of the pull cord or on the light switch.

11. How to Safely Mail Snapshots.

To send a snapshot through the mail without bending or breaking its edges, paste photograph corners—the kind used in albums—on a piece of cardboard slightly larger than picture. Insert picture inside these corners.

12. Soap Shavings.

Slit a sponge and insert soap shavings. Glue slit together and you have a handy soap-wash outfit.

13. Making Suction Cups Hold.

You will have no trouble keeping suction cups in place if you first rub the edge of the cup over a wet cake of soap.

14. "Recycle" Old Washcloths.

When washcloths become thin, stitch two together around the edges and you'll be surprised at how much more wear you can get from them.

15. Use of Luggage.

If space is at a premium, use the area inside unused luggage. Pack your best towels, pillowcases, gowns, or pajamas in the bags along with a few bars of unwrapped soap. This will give more storage space in drawers and linen closet, will keep the stored items smelling sweet, and will prevent the suitcases from developing a musty odor.

16. Aspirin Box as Stamp Holder.

An aspirin box makes an excellent stamp holder. Slip one in your stationery box and another in purse to make stamps easy to find and handle.

17. Felt on Chairs.

Glue thin strips of felt to the bottoms of dining-chair legs to prevent scratching hardwood floors.

18. When Mailing a Package. . .

dampen the string before tying. The string shrinks as it dries, making a safer and more securely tied package.

19. Cover Up for Nail Holes.

Tack and nail holes in light-colored wallpaper can be covered with a little dry cornstarch.

20. To Camouflage Nicks.

Rub small nicks in black wrought-iron furniture with a black crayon to camouflage the damaged spot temporarily.

21. To Prevent Snags.

It's a good idea to use a coat of enamel on the inside of bureau drawers as protection against snagging.

22. Make Own Shopping Bag.

Before starting out to shop, slip the top of a shoe box into the bottom of your shopping bag to reinforce it. Place the lid topside up so it will form a tray in the bag.

23. If you get a scald or burn, put vanilla on it as soon as possible, and it won't blister or smart.

24. Cotton on Mousetraps!

Cotton is good for baiting mousetraps, as mice like it for nesting. Put the cotton in and around the trap.

25. Outsmart That Mouse.

Want to outsmart that leery mouse. Put cheese on the trap about three nights without setting it, then bait and set it. You'll fool him and catch him sure.

26. Keep Cork from Sticking.

To prevent the cork in a glue bottle from sticking, dip it in melted paraffin and let it dry the first time you use it.

27. Save Electricity.

When leaving home for a weekend, set your refrigerator down to the lowest point, but not to defrost. Never place a refrigerator near a stove or heat appliance.

28. Blanket Protection.

Before storing blankets, add one cup of mothballs to the rinse water when they are washing. Discourages moths.

29. Crocheted Blanket Binding.

You can make your own blanket binding with a ten cent ball of crochet cotton. Crochet a neat edge at top and bottom to replace worn binding.

30. Cover Bed Springs.

Make a cover of unbleached domestic for bed springs; it will protect your sheets, and save cleaning of the springs.

31. Glue from store labels that remains on glassware can be removed by dabbing the area with transparent tape.

32. Cleaning Under Dresser.

You can often remove the bottom drawer of a bureau to clean the floor under the furniture rather than moving the bureau.

33. To Remove Decals. . .

from a wall or furniture, dip a cotton ball in boiling vinegar and sponge the decal with it—sponge until decal is thoroughly soaked, then simply wash the decal away.

34. Use of Egg Cartons.

To make an inexpensive jewelry box for a young girl, spray-paint an egg carton.

35. Roll Up Tea Towels.

More tea towels may be stored in a drawer by rolling them up. Also, it is easier to reach in and pick out the towel of your choice.

36. Avoid Sore Fingers From Thumbtacks. . .

by wearing a thimble on your pushing finger. Job is made easier and quicker.

37. Lighten a Dark Closet. . .

by painting the inside with a glossy white enamel.

38. When Packing a Fragile Item. . .

for mailing, place it inside a plastic bag and inflate the bag as you would a ballon. The air pocket helps protect the item against breakage.

39. If Curtains Hang Crooked. . .

put an extra rod through the bottom hem for a time.

40. Paintbrush Use.

Purchase a 2-inch-wide paintbrush. Dust wood shutters, grandfather's clock, picture frames, carvings on furniture, figurines, rungs on chairs, wicker furniture, lamp shades, cut glass, chandeliers, silk flowers, windowsills. . . .just a few of the many uses for this item.

41. Bedspread Substitute.

Substitute colored sheets for bedspreads when you have a sick patient in bed for an extended time. This not only saves wear and tear on the more expensive bedspreads; it also saves wear and tear on you, for they are easier to handle and to launder.

42. To Remove Transparent Tape

from paper or cardboard without marring the surface, run a warm iron over the tape to soften the adhesive. Then gently pull off tape.

43. A Good Deodorizer.

Leave a bottle of lemon juice uncorked in the bathroom. It's a good deodorizer.

44. Protect Tape-Measure Numbers.

To prevent numbers from wearing off a flexible steel tape measure, cover the tape with transparent tape.

45. Handy Shoe Rack.

Make a handy shoe rack by tacking a curtain rod on the closet door. Hang shoes by the heel over it.

46. Don't Mar Tables With Bookends.

Glue pieces of heavy felt cloth to the bottoms of bookends to keep them from marring tables or bookshelves.

47. Moisten Stamps With Glue Bottle.

Fill an empty glue bottle with water and use it to moisten stamps and seal envelopes. The rubber top on the bottle will spread the water sparingly and evenly.

48. Restore Cedar Odor.

When a cedar chest loses its odor, it can be restored by sanding the interior lightly with fine sandpaper.

49. How to Grip Water Bottle.

Keep a few wide rubber bands around a hot or cold bottle. This will give a better grip on the bottle and lesson the chance of dropping it.

50. Paint Odor.

If you will put a few tablespoons of vanilla in a cup of water and let it stand in the room where there is fresh paint, it will dispel the paint odor.

51. To help dirt slide off your dust pan, try waxing it with a no-rub liquid wax.

52. Warmth Without Weight.

For extra warmth without weight, put a sheet of 54 inch plastic between two blankets.

53. Joining Card Tables.

When forming a long table with card tables, join the legs together with large rubber bands, and prevent them separating.

54. Homemade Soft Soap.

Save scraps of soap. To every cupful add a cup of boiling water, simmer over slow heat until dissolved. Put in a container and cool. This soap has many uses. Dissolved in lukewarm water it can be used for washing lingerie or for a shampoo.

55. Care of Books.

Never crowd books into shelves; it breaks the bindings. Bookshelves should be built away from open registers or glaring sun, which warps the binding and also fades.

56. To Hold a Candle Securely. . .

melt some paraffin, or a bit of the bottom of the candle into the holder, and insert the candle while hot.

57. Long Life for Candles.

Candles will burn evenly and not

drip, if chilled in the refrigerator 24 hours before using.

58. Double the Wear of Sheets.

When bed sheets begin to wear thin in the middle, tear down the center, and sew the selvaged edges together, then hem the torn edges, double the life of your sheets.

59. A lump of sugar placed in the teapot before making tea prevents its staining the tablecloth if spilled.

60. Remedy for Large Screw Holes.

When a screw hole is too large or worn to hold the screw, it may be remedied by breaking a wooden kitchen match and shoving it in the hole, then screwing the screw in place. It will hold as though it is part of the wood of the object.

61. For Pretty Tiebacks. . .

for bedroom curtains, use pop beads that match your color scheme or ones that contrast nicely.

62. Take Itch Out of Mosquito Bites. . .

with antacid tablets. Just moisten a tablet and rub on the bite. Since the acid in the bite causes the itch, the antacid neutralizes it and stops the irritation.

63. Stuck Water Glasses.

You can pull apart two glasses that are stuck if first you set the bottom one in warm water and then pour cold water in the top one.

64. To Mend a Tear in a Sheer Curtain. . .

apply clear fingernail polish and press the edges together each time you launder them.

65. Many Uses for Foam Rubber.

Buy by the yard and use. . .
A. A large piece placed carefully in your bed can often help a backache.
B. Small pieces in shoes can keep the shoes from hurting.
C. Wonderful for packing material for precious, breakable items you are mailing.
D. A piece of foam rubber the size of your suitcase is great to carry on a trip to keep things in place.
E. A good substitute to use to put on loose powder or rouge.

66. Fair Shake.

Hate to clean your blender? Simply fill it half full of water and add a small amount of detergent. Turn it on for a second, then rinse with hot water. The blender will be clean and shining.

67. When hanging pictures, heat the nail and it will not chip or crack the plaster.

68. If you criss-cross the wires of your pictures before hanging them, they will not shift nor slip out of place.

69. Hanging Pictures.

To hang a heavy picture or mirror, you can find the stud, with the aid of a compass, which will be attracted to the nails, thus showing the exact location of the studs.

70. A round corn pad glued to each corner of a picture frame on the back will keep the picture from sliding around when you are ready to hang it on the wall.

71. To Keep Pictures Hanging Staight. . .

paste a small piece of sandpaper on the back of the picture near the bottom.

72. To remove crayon marks from wallpaper, take a dry cloth sprinkled with dry Dutch cleanser and rub the spot.

73. A pocket sewn on the inside of a shower curtain will hold a cake of soap within easy reach.

74. Duplicate Those Credit Cards, etc.

Using a copying machine, make a visual record of wallet contents—credit cards, driver's license, charge plates, etc.—on a sheet of paper to insure prompt and accurate reporting in case of loss or theft.

75. When going on a picnic, put hot dogs in a wide-mouthed vacuum bottle and fill with boiling water. The franks will be ready to eat by the time the picnic spot is reached.

76. Thumbtack Picnic Tablecloths.

Take plenty of thumbtacks along when going on an outdoor picnic. If

a brisk wind comes up, you can use the tacks not only to fasten down the tablecloth but the paper plates as well.

77. Wrapping a piece of adhesive tape around the center of the wire on the back of a picture will prevent it from slipping on the hook or nail.

78. If you starch your ironing board cover, your clothes will iron much nicer.

SEWING HINTS

79. Glue Down Tape Measure.

Glue a length of tape measure to the front of the sewing machine where it is always handy for the many short measurements necessary when sewing.

80. That Pesky Zipper!

If you have a zipper that is forever coming open, sew a small matching button to the garment at the top of the zipper. Draw a loop made of strong thread through the hole in the zipper pull. When you zip up the garment, fasten the hoop over the button.

81. Never press woolen fabrics dry because too much heat damages the fibers.

82. Turn Collars With Letter Opener.

Keep a plastic letter opener near the sewing machine. You will find it ideal to use when turning collars and cuffs.

83. Stuffing Toys.

Worn-out nylon hose cut into small pieces make soft, easy-to-wash stuffing for animals and small stuffed toys.

84. Darning Gloves.

A marble makes a fine darning egg when mending the fingers of a glove.

85. Footstool Protector.

To keep your footstools easy to clean, use a piece of clear plastic sheet right over the material the next time you cover the stool.

86. Uses for Old Shirts.

Worn men's shirts can be made into underwear, pajamas, aprons or blouses. Buttoned down the back they can be made into smocks.

87. New Collars and Cuffs.

Get new wear out of old dresses by adding new collars and cuffs. Make them from scraps in your sewing box, or buy them ready-made.

88. Make a Jumper.

Often an ill-fitting dress can be made into a smooth-fitting jumper to wear with different blouses. Cut out sleeves, lower the neckline, and narrow the shoulders.

89. Turn the Collar.

When men's shirt collars become worn, don't discard, turn the collar and get twice the wear.

90. Stitching Nylon.

When stitching on synthetic materials, such as dacron and nylon, decrease your machine tension, and you will get a smooth stitch.

91. Cover for Washer.

If your automatic washer is in the kitchen, make a fitted cover for it of clear plastic, get protection for the washer, make an extra table, discourage small fry from opening the door.

92. Padding for Pot Holders.

The good portions of worn-out bath towels make fine padding for pot holders. They are soft and easy to handle, and launder well.

93. Save That Bottom Button.

Reduce the strain on the bottom button of your button-down-the-front dress by sewing the last button on an inch of elastic, it will stretch and save tearing the dress.

94. Buy Extra Material.

When buying material for young children's clothes, buy an extra half yard. When extra alterations or mending become necessary you will have the necessary material.

95. To Lengthen Pajamas.

When children's pajamas become too short, lengthen sleeves and legs with the ribbed part of a worn sock. It will lengthen, make a neat finish, add wear and warmth.

96. To Clean a Sewing Machine.

Give your old sewing machine a thorough cleaning with kerosene, clean every moving part, and wipe dry. Apply a little sewing machine oil. Stitch thru a blotter or an old piece of cloth a few times to soak up any excess oil.

97. Magnet in Sewing Basket.

A small magnet placed in your sewing basket will save you lots of time in picking up needles and pins that you drop to the floor.

98. New Comforter.

A new comforter can be made from those old blankets. Stitch two or three together and cover with a pretty cotton print.

99. Threading Needle.

Make it easier to thread a sewing-machine needle by slipping a piece of white paper underneath the needle. This shows up the eye of the needle.

100. Temporary Relief for Hem Rip.

If a hem rips out while you are away from home, a strip of cellophane tape will hold it in place, saving you embarrassment.

101. To Pick Up Thread.

Use thoroughly dampened facial tissues to pick up sewing threads or broken glass from the floor.

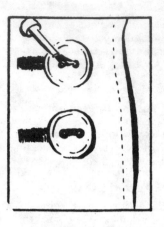

102. Scissors Sharpener.

To sharpen scissors, you have only to cut thru a piece of sandpaper a few times.

103. Sewing Slippery Material.

To prevent slippage when sewing slippery materials on the machine, pin a turkish towel or crib sheet to the leaf of the sewing machine. It really works.

104. Keep a candle in your sewing machine drawer. Draw end of thread through candle wax and you'll have no trouble threading that needle.

105. Have Another Button Handy.

When you make a dress, we suggest you sew a button on the underside to match those on the dress, then when one is lost, you won't have to rummage around for a look-alike!

106. Cover Button With Nail Polish.

If you will touch the center of each button on a new garment with transparent nail polish, it will seal the threads and will not ravel.

107. "Hefty" Apron.

Make a quick apron for those messy jobs by cutting holes in a large plastic garbage bag for your arms and head.

CLOTHING

And

Its

Care

108. Shaving Cream Cleaner.

Everyone gets stains on carpets, but not everyone removes them with shaving cream. I do because it contains soap and water and it's right there in a handy container. Just squirt it on and rub it in with a soft brush. Blot up with water and paper towels. I find this is effective even on old stains! Caution: Before you use this or any other stain remover on your carpet, test it on an out-of-sight spot.

109. Sandpaper Fuzz Balls.

To keep nylon and orlon sweaters looking neat and presentable, try sandpapering off all fuzz balls.

110. Shine on Navy Blue.

Remove the shine from navy blue material by sponging it with undiluted vinegar. Both odor and shine will be removed as the material dries.

111. Discolored Handkerchiefs

may be whitened by soaking them in cold water to which a pinch of cream of tartar has been added.

112. To Eliminate Wrinkles. . .

keep a wash-and-wear garment on a hanger, even when soiled and waiting to be laundered. Not only will this eliminate wrinkles but it helps hold the garment's natural shape.

113. Brush Clothes Before Storing.

Before storing woolens, brush before placing in storage box. Shake ordinary table salt generously over the articles, then store in a dry place. The salt absorbs moisture that is often attracted to woolens. When you are ready to wear the garment again, just shake off the salt. The articles will be clean and odorless.

114. Store Small Woolens. . .

like gloves, scarves and sweaters for the summer in clean fruit jars; add some moth crystals and seal.

115. To Freshen Velvet. . .

garment, hang it over a large kettle of boiling water for a few minutes. Then brush with a piece of velvet until the nap is raised again.

116. To Hold Sweaters in Shape . . .

before washing, lay it out flat on a piece of brown paper and draw an outline. After washing and when ready to dry, lay it within the outline, stretch and pat to fit the outline; it will dry in the exact size.

117. Cloves to Repel Mice.

Mice do not like whole cloves, so pack cloves with clothing to repel those pesky little rodents and also to keep clothing from developing musty odors.

118. Nail Polish on Coat Hangers.

A coating of clear fingernail polish is good for those wire coathangers on which you hang garments made of sheer materials.

119. Wrap rubber bands around the ends of your clothes hangers to prevent the garments from slipping.

120. Starch Scarfs and Blouses.

Silk scarfs and old silk blouses will get new life if they are dipped in a very light starch and ironed while damp.

121. Before Washing Socks. . .

safety pin pairs at the toe in a family where sizes and color are similar and confusing. This saves time when washing and drying clothes.

122. Dental Floss for Sewing on Buttons.

If buttons on winter coats fall off more often than usual, try sewing them on with dental floss. This is stronger than normal thread and will hold the button even under heavy stress conditions.

123. Washing Leather Gloves.

Leather gloves can be laundered at home (not chamois or suede) washed on the hands in cool suds. Roll down from the wrist, do not pull by fingers while wet. Squeeze out water without twisting. Place away from heat to dry.

124. Reinforcing Rubber Gloves.

Rubber gloves usually develop leaks in the same spot—first and second finger or thumb—while the remainder of the glove is in fine shape. So reinforce by turning the glove inside out and applying a strip of adhesive tape to their vulnerable spots before use.

125. Protect Those Rubber Gloves.

Bits of cotton pushed into the finger tips of rubber gloves will keep long finger nails from cutting through the rubber.

126. Care of Rubber Goods.

Rubber goods such as swim caps, gloves, etc. will not stick together if covered with a little cornstarch or talcum powder, inside and out, when stored. Keep in a cool place.

127. Those Odd Nylon Stockings

can be rematched and worn after they have been boiled in water for 10 minutes. The stockings all become the same shade.

128. Dying Hose.

Collect all unmatched or odd hose, get a package of color remover from the dime store, and remove color, then tint in one shade.

129. Longer Wear for Hose.

For longer wear of hose, wash after each wearing in lukewarm water and mild soap. Be sure they are completely dry before wearing.

130. Choosing Material.

When buying a new garment, check the labels; buy color-fast, pre-

shrunk materials, and save yourself money and time.

131. Clear nail polish applied to pearl buttons restores the gloss.

132. Remove Perspiration Odors

from garments by rubbing over stained area with a solution of one part ammonia and eight parts water.

133. For Less Cleaning Bills. . .

brush clothing thoroughly and often. Upholstery attachment on vacuum makes a fine brush for woolen clothing.

134. Not a Shred Left.

What do you do if you accidentally wash a tissue with your clothing, and tissue shreds and clings to fabric? I put everything in the dryer with a couple of fabric softener sheets, and most of the paper mess comes off. Use a clothes brush to remove any lint that remains.

135. How to Dry Furs.

Never dry a wet fur near a heater or radiator. Shake well and hang in a cool place.

136. Avoid Friction of Furs.

Friction ages your furs more rapidly than any other cause. Avoid frequent carrying of books and bundles, and driving long distances in your fur coat.

137. Wear a Scarf.

Save on cleaning bills by wearing a scarf at your neck; protects collar from powder and cream.

138. Leakproof Your Raincoat.

You can leakproof your raincoat, when you get a tear, with adhesive tape pressed on the tear on the underneath side.

139. Storing Hats.

Before packing hats away for the season, remove veil and fragile trimming. Cover well with tissue paper, and keep from light and dust.

140. To Renew a Veil. . .

press over a sheet of waxed paper.

141. Brighten Up Old Felt.

Brighten up an old felt hat by holding it over a steaming pot of water. Brush with a soft brush while still damp.

142. Spot Remover.

To remove a spot of oil or grease sprinkle it with talcum powder. After several hours, when it has absorbed the grease, brush it off. Repeat if necessary.

143. Cleaner for White Felt.

Make a paste of flour and gasoline to clean a white felt hat. Rub paste into the felt and hang in the air.

144. To Store a Handbag. . .

stuff with crumpled tissue paper. This helps bag hold its shape. Place in a plastic bag and close with a rubber band. This keeps it dust free.

145. Protection for Leather Bags.

An application of liquid wax on leather bags not only protects the bag, but prevents color from rubbing off on clothing.

146. Moths Like Fabrics of Animal Origin.

Moths damage only fabrics of animal origin such as fur, feathers, wool and hair. When you buy clothing of cotton, linen and rayon you have no moth problems.

147. Moth Protection.

To protect articles from moths, launder or dry clean first; grease spots are attacked by moths first of all. Then place in a box, trunk or chest between layers of tissue paper and moth crystals. Seal tightly every crack with gummed tape.

148. Care of Patents.

Remove smudges from patent leather shoes by rubbing with a small amount of petroleum jelly applied with a soft cloth.

149.

Use window cleaner to spiff up your "tired" patent leathers.

150.

Use liquid self-polishing floor

wax to preserve the finish on the new wet-look footwear.

151. Heel Cushion for Shoe.

When an extra heel cushion is needed for your shoe, cut it from one side of a powder puff.

152. To Remove Grease Spots From Suede Leather. . .

rub with a piece of matching colored chalk. Let set, then brush carefully with a suede brush or sponge.

153. Emery Board and Suede Shoes.

Bring new life to suede shoes by rubbing them with a fine emery board. The board will restore the suede nap, making the shoes look new again.

154. Nail Polish on Leather Hells.

Keep leather heels on shoes bright and shiny by giving them an occasional coat of colorless nail polish.

155. Slip Boots on Easily.

Dust baby powder in your boots before putting them on and see how easily they slip on and off.

156. Storing Shoes.

When storing out-of-season shoes, prevent mildew from forming on them by applying a thin coat of wax to entire shoe, including soles.

157. Shoe Care.

Air your shoes a day between wearings, and double the life of your shoes. Perspiration rots linings and leather.

158. Sandpaper Slick Soles. . .

to prevent accidents by slipping on slick pavements.

159. To Keep Wet Shoes Soft. . .

apply saddle soap before drying. Never dry in direct heat. Stuff full of paper while drying to hold shape.

160. Make New Sandals.

When leather sandals become scuffed, paint a bright color; when dry, cover with colorless nail polish to protect the paint.

COOKING

HINTS

161. A teaspoon of flour added to sugar when making candy or cake frosting will always give a smooth and creamy substance.

162. No-Lump Gravy.

To make easier gravy, put the flour and 3 or 4 oz. of water in a half-pint jar and shake quickly. Then pour into hot fat in the skillet. It will not get lumpy.

163. If you happen to have too much grease in your gravy, take the greasy film away by stirring in a little cream.

164. To Remove Insects From Vegetables. . .

which are being washed, put some vinegar or a pinch of salt in the water. This will bring live insects to the surface pronto.

165. Prevent Soggy Salad.

To prevent a vegetable salad from becoming sodden when it has to stand, place a saucer upside down in the bowl before filling it with salad. The moisture will run underneath and the salad will remain crisp and fresh.

166. Care of Celery.

Celery is 94 per cent water, and it needs moisture and to be kept cold to remain fresh. So before refrigerating a stalk, run cold water over it, let excess water drip off and place the stalk in a plastic bag or container with a tight lid to prevent circulating air from pulling moisture out of the celery cells.

167. Draw Out Burn from Beans.

If beans should happen to burn while cooking, place a dry slice of bread on top of beans and it will draw all the burnt taste out. Then exchange pans and keep on cooking.

168. Ice Cube Fudge!

Pour fudge into buttered ice cube trays: it hardens quickly and every piece is uniform in size.

169. Marshmallow Icing.

When baking cupcakes try placing a marshmallow on the top of each cake just before removing from oven. You will have a nice tasty frosting without bother.

170. If you will add a tablespoon of vinegar to the fat that you fry doughnuts in, the doughnut will not absorb the grease.

171. When frying doughnuts, try putting a few whole cloves in the kettle of fat for a nice flavor.

172. Add A Little Cocoa!

For chocolate cakes or cookies that call for a greased and floured pan, add a little cocoa to the flour. The finished cake or cookies won't have that floury look.

173. In Making a Cake. . .

always cream the flavoring spice, or grated fruit peel with the shortening. The aromatic flavor is then mixed more thoroughly through the batter.

174. When rolling out sugar cookies, use powdered sugar on your board instead of flour. Cookies have

much better flavor and don't get hard.

175. Testing Eggs.

When in doubt about their freshness, test eggs in a pan of cold water. An egg that floats is bad; one that stands on end is stale; one that lies at an angle should be used immediately or discarded; one that lies flat is fresh.

176. Don't Break Yolk!

A sharp knife that has been dipped in hot water will slice hard-cooked eggs without breaking the yolks.

177. Don't Crack That Egg!

Dip eggs in ice water before boiling, then they will not crack.

178. Cracked Eggs.

To boil eggs that have been cracked, add a teaspoon of salt to the water. Salt causes egg white to set quickly.

179. Beating Eggs.

Eggs beat up lighter, and make lighter cakes when used at room temperature.

180. Simmer Hard-Boiled Eggs.

"Hard-boiled" eggs will be tastier, and better if simmered 15 minutes, and not boiled.

181. When boiling eggs for later use, add a little food coloring to the water. When you store with un-cooked eggs in refrigerator, tint tells the difference.

182. Prevent Cracked Shell.

Before hard-cooking eggs, pierce the rounded end with a needle. The shells will not crack while cooking and peeling will be easier.

183. To separate the egg white from the yolk, break the egg over a small funnel. The white will glide through; the yolk will remain.

184. Making Quick Hamburgers.

When entertaining friends at a hamburger fry, try rolling out the hamburger steak to the desired thickness with a rolling pin, placing the meat between layers of waxed paper so it will not stick. Cut with biscuit cutter. Much quicker than the usual way of making patties.

185. Freezing Hamburger Patties.

To save on aluminum foil, freeze hamburger patties in the plastic lids of 1-lb. coffee cans. Put a small piece of waxed paper between each one when freezing. Lids can be washed and reused.

186. Hamburgers in Foil.

Cover your grill with aluminum foil when cooking hamburgers. They will cook fine and you will have no messy pans to wash.

187. When using hamburger for meat loaf, add a grated raw potato. This makes it juicy and softer, in addition to giving it an extra good flavor.

188. When frying hamburgers on top of the stove, dip them in milk before putting in pan; and they will brown nicely.

189. Perk Up Those Chops!

A dash of celery salt and a sprinkle of brown sugar is a delightful change for pork chops.

190. Use Thimble When Grating.

Wear a thimble over thumb when grating vegetables. This protects the thumb from nicks and also protects the manicure.

191. Drop a thimble over the center tube in a percolator before adding ground coffee; filling the pot will be easier with no worry about grounds falling into the water.

192. Perk Up Tired Lemons!

When lemons become dry, put in a warm oven for a few seconds and see them become plump and juicy again.

193. Keeping Lemons.

You can keep them for months by putting them whole into sterilized jars covered with cold water. Adjust rubber rings and screw covers down tightly.

194. Add Egg to Mash Potatoes.

Mashed potatoes improve in texture and taste with the addition of a beaten egg white. They will whip up lighter if the milk is hot when you add it.

195.

If you get too much salt in your potatoes, simply add a little sugar; and to modify the sweetness of something, add a little salt.

196. Add Applesauce to Sweet Potatoes.

You can vary a sweet-potato dish by blending 1 part sweetened applesauce with 3 parts cooked sweet potatoes. Season to taste.

197. Eat the Whole Potato.

The most valuable vitamins and minerals of a potato are found in the skin itself, so eat the whole potato.

198. Keep Sandwiches Fresh. . .

longer by sealing the edges of the wax paper, in which you wrap them, with a hot iron.

199. Substitute for Whipped Cream.

You will have a delicious substitute for whipped cream by adding one banana to two eggs whites and beating until stiff. (The banana will dissolve.) Add 2 tbs. sugar.

200. Frozen Whipped Cream.

Left-over whipped cream can be frozen. Cover a tray with waxed paper. Drop the whipped cream in large spoonfuls. Place in freezer until frozen. When frozen solid, store in a sealed plastic bag. Allow 15 minutes for thawing.

201. Good Popcorn.

If popcorn isn't popping as it should, add 3 tablespoons of water and keep it in the refrigerator until you're ready to use it. It works wonders.

202.

To shave chocolate quickly, use a potato peeler.

203.

If your soup is too salty, put a piece of raw potato in it. The potato will absorb the salt.

204.

Thicken soups with 2 or 3 tablespoons of oatmeal. . .adds richness and flavor. Barley or rice are good, too.

205.

Shredded coconut may be freshened by soaking in milk a few moments before using.

206. Baking Green Peppers.

Green peppers will retain their coloring longer if brushed with olive oil before stuffed and baked—and they are shaped better when baked in muffin tins.

207. Scallop for Cucumber.

Run the tines of a fork lengthwise over a peeled cucumber, then slice and get an attractive scalloped edge.

208. Rust on Lettuce.

To prevent "rust" on lettuce when storing in refrigerator, wrap in paper towels.

209. For Fluffy Rice. . .

add a teaspoon of lemon juice to each quart of water used in cooking. Cook without a cover.

210. Vinegar on Rice!

If a teaspoon of vinegar is added to the cup of rice when it is cooking, the kernels will be chalk white and the rice will not stick to the bottom of the pot. This will help, too, in making the kernels stay apart.

211. Soak Dried Beans and Cereal.

It takes less fuel to cook dried beans, cereal and fruit, if they are first soaked a few hours in cold water.

212. Double Boiler Trick.

While the vegetables cook in the bottom of the double boiler, make the sauce in the top part, and save fuel.

213. Keep Apples Bright.

To prevent apples from turning brown as you peel them, drop into cold, lightly-salted water.

214. Perfect Baked Apples.

Apples can be baked without cracking and every bit of flavor retained if a one-inch band is peeled from the middle of each apple. Stuff the apple and bake in a moderate oven.

215. Pastry Shell Idea.

Spread one-half cup of uncooked rice in the bottom of your pastry shell while cooking to keep it in shape. Rice can be used over and over again.

216. Dessert Stretcher.

Make an attractive and delicious dessert by adding cubes of bright colored jello to a fruit cup.

217. Toasted Coconut.

Stale coconut can be toasted in a very low oven till golden brown and used in the same manner as fresh coconut.

218. Fry for Dieters, Too.

If you are frying chicken for the family and one person is dieting, a simple way to cut calories is to wrap his or her portion (unbreaded) securely in aluminum foil and place in cooking fat along with the rest, turning it as you turn the rest. It will cook at the same time with no extra fuss.

219. Cut Down on Calories. . .

in confectioners sugar icing by substituting one fourth powdered milk for that much sugar, sift the two together. Makes an interesting flavor also.

220. Protect Vitamins and Minerals.

Most vegetables should be cooked in the smallest possible quantity of water. Saves fuel and valuable vitamins and minerals.

221. To Toast Marshmallows. . .

dip the fork in butter first; this prevents sticking.

222. Buy Day-Old Bread. . .

which is cheaper and makes better toast than fresh bread.

223. To Freshen Stale Rolls. . .

and muffins, sprinkle with water, place in a paper bag and heat in a slow oven a few minutes.

224. Use of Stale Bread.

Use stale bread by making croutons. Cut them into cubes, sprinkle with garlic powder, put in 250-degree oven. After 20 minutes turn off oven and leave in pan in oven for an hour or so.

225. Leftover Rolls.

Warm leftover rolls by placing in a dampened brown paper bag and baking in a medium-heated oven for 10 minutes. The rolls should be just as fluffy as when first baked.

226. How to Warm Over Rolls.

The foil-insulated bags used for ice cream are great to put rolls in when you warm them up at suppertime.

227. Banish Onion Odor. . .

from hands by washing them with chlorophyll toothpaste instead of soap.

228. Dealing With Onion Fumes.

The next time you slice onions, and before peeling, hold a one-inch chunk of bread between your teeth. The bread will absorb the fumes.

229. Onion Breath.

After eating raw onions, eat a few sprigs of parsley dipped in salt or vinegar to avoid the smell of onions on your breath.

230. Shred the Butter.

When a recipe calls for softened butter but you have forgotten to take it out of the refrigerator in advance, measure the correct amount and shred it as you would a carrot. The small pieces will be soft enough to work with immediately.

231. Eggs-actly the Same.

When you're short one egg for a cake mix calling for two eggs or more, substitute two tablespoons of mayonnaise. You'll never taste the difference.

232. Brown Bag Ice Cubes.

A day or two before a party, I begin making extra ice cubes. But I put the cubes in brown paper bags (instead of plastic) and they never stick together.

233. Lumps in Sugar?

You can remove them from powdered and brown sugar by placing the sugar in a warm oven for just a few minutes.

234. Don't Salt Roast Beef. . .

until it is 75 per cent done, some cooks advise, since salt draws out the juices and flavor.

235. Add to Biscuits.

Did you ever try serving breakfast biscuits made with orange or pineapple juice instead of milk? Great.

236. Those Strings on Beans!

If you are having difficulty removing those strings, try your potato peeler. Just run it right along the edge of the bean and you will be surprised at how easily those strings come off.

237. Paring Grapefruit Lining.

To loosen the white lining of grapefruit, pour boiling water over whole grapefruit and let stand a few seconds before paring.

238. Storing Cookies.

Place a piece of lemon peel in the cookie jar before you put in those freshly baked cookies for storage; the cookies will stay fresh and crisp longer.

239. Cooking Spinach.

Never add water to spinach when cooking, the water which clings to the leaves is quite sufficient. Cook ten to twelve minutes.

240. Substitute for Spinach.

Beet tops make a fine substitute for spinach.

241. Help for Hulling Walnuts.

Pour boiling water over walnuts that are to be cracked and let stand about one-half hour. They will break easier and the nutmeats will come out in larger pieces.

242. Handy Pop Corn Popper.

You can use your pressure cooker, without gauge, for popping corn. The cover fits tightly, cooker is heavy and will not burn easily.

243. Angel Meat Loaf

To vary meat loaf, try cooking it in an angel food pan. Unmold on a large plate, and fill center with creamed vegetables. A meal in one dish.

244. Vanilla-Wafer Pie Shells.

If you make pie shells from vanilla wafers, save time by crushing a whole box and store in a covered jar until needed.

245. Cooking Sausages.

Link sausages will shrink less and not pop open if boiled in water about three minutes before frying.

246. Whip Evaporated Milk.

Make ice cream and toppings for cake with evaporated milk. To whip well, both bowl and milk must be thoroughly chilled.

247. To Make Sour Milk. . .

add two teaspoons of vinegar to a cup of sweet milk and stir.

248. Prepare Nutmeats.

To prepare chopped nutmeats for baking, place them in a clean cloth and run a rolling pin over them.

249. Chicken rolled in powdered milk instead of flour will fry to a golden brown.

250. Roll Bacon First.

Before opening a package of bacon, roll it into a tube. That loosens the slices and keeps them from sticking together.

251. Never Heat the Oven for Just One Dish.

Plan your meal so that you never heat the oven for one dish only. Make a complete meal at the same time, whenever possible.

252. Cookbook Protector.

Cover the pages of the cookbook

with a sheet of clear plastic, and avoid splashes and greasy finger prints.

253. Safe Travel for Pies.

To carry that pie safely to the picnic, place an empty pie pan over it, and fasten the two together with cellophane tape.

254. Molded Salad Variation.

If your family is small, vary molded salad by making half a box of Jello into vegetable salad and the other half into fruit salad for another day.

KITCHEN CARE

255. Keeping Drains Unclogged.

Keep those drains free-flowing by pouring one cup of baking soda into the drain every week. Follow it by pouring in one cup of vinegar. As the soda and vinegar foam up, flush the drain with about a quart of boiling water. That should do it!

256. Put Sponge in Soap Dish.

If you will place small pieces of sponge in soap dishes for economy, they will keep the soap firm and dry but will retain enough soap for washing the sink or lavatory.

257. Powder Puff in Flour Canister!

Keep an inexpensive powder puff in your flour canister to use when dusting cake pans, pastry board, and cookie sheets. The flour will be more evenly distributed and there's no waste.

258. Use of Embroidery Hoop.

An old embroidery hoop makes a good hanger for kitchen towel, keeping it off the floor and within reach. Slip a cord through the ring and hang it in a handy place near the kitchen sink.

259. Cleaning Tea Kettle.

To get lime deposits off inside of tea kettle, boil in it water to which cream of tartar has been added.

* * *

260. Reduce Utensil Washing Time.

Get a plastic container approximately five inches in diameter and five inches in height. Fill the bottom with clean water when cooking and set it in corner of sink. Put your cooking tools and silverware in it rather than leave them around to dry while cooking. It reduces utensil washing time.

261.

Put a revolving tie rack near the kitchen sink for hanging brushes, measuring spoons and other small utensils.

262. Care of Lunch Boxes.

Loose rice placed in the bottom of a lunch box before the napkin is placed in it will keep the box from becoming damp.

263. Container for Fat.

A discarded coffee percolator makes a great container for fat or meat fryings. The coffee basket may be used to strain the fats, and the pot itself will hold the fat.

264. To Prevent Grease from Spattering. . .

and splashing on the stove when frying meat, place a piece of bread in the pan. This cuts down cleaning the stove.

265. Care of Scouring Pads.

After using steel wool scouring pads, wrap them in aluminum foil. This prevents any dripping or rusting until they are used again.

266. Save on Scouring Pads.

Instead of using a whole scouring pad for a small, badly-burned pan, crumble a small piece of aluminum foil and use that with a bit of scouring powder.

267. Discolored Meat or Bread Boards. . .

become clean again if they are rubbed with lemon rinds turned inside out, then washed with warm water and rubbed dry with a soft cloth.

268. Fuel Saver.

Using pans smaller than the burner is a waste of fuel. Use a flat bottom pan the same size, or larger than the burner.

269. Thrifty Potato Peeler.

For a quick, thrifty potato peeler, or for turnips or carrots, use a metal sponge.

270. Milk Cartons for Garbage Containers.

Empty milk cartons make excellent little garbage containers. Being moisture proof they keep the garbage pail clean and dry.

271. Tip for Broiling.

Put half a cup of water in the broiler, when broiling steaks or other meat, it will prevent the fat from burning, and also make good gravy.

272. Oil With Glycerin.

To lubricate egg beaters and similar kitchen utensils, use tasteless, odorless, harmless glycerin instead of machine oil.

273. Cooling Oven Quickly.

If you bake early on summer days and wish to quickly cool the oven, then place a pan of cold water on a rack.

274. Cleaning the Oven.

Never wash the inside of your oven while hot. Let it cool thoroughly and wash with hot soap suds, rinse and dry well.

275. Cleaning an Electric Skillet.

To clean the bottom of an electric skillet, heat and spray with oven cleaner. Then watch all the burned-on grease wipe off. You can clean an iron skillet by same method.

276. When Food Boils Over. . .

on the electric range, turn heat to high and burn it off. When cool, take a soft brush and brush out the charred particles.

277. Cleaning Kitchen Appliances.

For a quick, effective job of cleaning a white kitchen stove, refrigerator, or white enameled cabinets, use spray-on-type window cleaner and rub with soft, clean cloth.

278. Baking Soda Versus Heel Marks and Burned-On Food.

Just three tablespoons of baking soda dissolved in one quart of warm water will make the kitchen sparkle again. The soda solution will remove heel marks from tile and linoleum floors and burned-on food from pots and pans. Sprinkle some baking soda on a damp sponge and scour those ugly rings and marks in the bathtub, shower stall, and bathroom sink. The same scouring motion may be used on tiles and chrome.

279. Towel on Refrigerator Door.

Pin a kitchen towel to the refrigerator handle. It is an excellent way to keep messy hands from smearing the refrigerator door.

280. Absorb Moisture.

A clean cellulose sponge kept in the vegetable bin of the refrigerator will absorb excess moisture.

281. Absorb Odors.

A peeled raw potato kept in the refrigerator will absorb all odors.

282. Refrigerator Freshener.

Keep your refrigerator fresh by washing it weekly with a weak solution of baking soda or borax.

283. Care for Ice Trays.

Wash ice trays with boiling water and a little bicarbonate of soda to keep them fresh.

284. Prevent Ice Cubes from Sticking. . .

by placing aluminum foil in bottom of ice cube trays.

Or

Cover the shelves of freezing compartment with waxed paper. Dry trays thoroughly before placing in refrigerator.

Or

Coat the outside bottom and sides of trays with floor wax.

285. Cleaning Woodenware.

Use as little water as possible on woodenware; clean immediately after each use. Keep away from heat or refrigeration.

286. Eliminate Fish Odors.

A little ammonia in the dishwater

will eliminate fish odors from dishes
and pans.

287. Cleaning the Teakettle.

The coating of lime which forms on
a teakettle can be removed by boiling a solution of vinegar and water
in the kettle a few minutes.

288. For Bright Aluminum.

Discoloration in aluminum cooking
vessels can be removed with a solution of two tablespoons cream of
tartar to a quart of water. Boil the
solution in the vessel 8 to 10
minutes.

289. Prevent Discoloration.

Put ½ teaspoon cream of tartar in
the lower part of an aluminum double boiler when in use, and it will
not become discolored.

290. Pattern for Table Setting.

Draw a picture of a complete place
setting on a paper place mat so that
your very young child can enjoy setting the table without asking questions.

LAUNDRY
and
Ironing
Helps

291. Ironing Board Cover.

The legs of old discarded pajamas double effectively as ironing board covers. They stay in place without tacking and are disposable.

292. Aluminum Foil Under Ironing Board Cover.

Lay a strip of heavy-duty aluminum foil the full length of your ironing board under the cover. Heat will reflect through the garment. This cuts ironing time almost in half and saves electricity and energy, too.

293. In Pressing Pleats.

When ironing or pressing pleats, snap a clothespin to the lower edge of the pleats until the garment is dry. The pleats will then hang flat and keep their shape longer.

294. Cornstarch for Scorched Article.

If you scorch an article while ironing, wet the piece and rub cornstarch into the scorched area. Allow it to dry and all traces of scorch will disappear. Only in the worst cases will you ever have to repeat the treatment.

295. Use Narrow End of Ironing Board.

When ironing flatwork, turn the ironing board so that the iron rests on the narrow end of the board. This give more ironing surface for the larger pieces.

296. Use of Piano Stool.

Paint an old-fashioned piano stool in your favorite color. You will find it very convenient for ironing, for it may be adjusted to any height.

297. Hydrogen peroxide helps remove scorch stains from garments. Apply immediately. Works especially well on woolens.

298. Sprinkling for Easy Ironing.

Sprinkle clothes for ironing with warm water; it will penetrate the fabric more quickly than cold water.

299. More Sprinkling Ideas.

After sprinkling, fold each piece lightly; tight crumpling makes extra wrinkles. Store in a cellophane bag with zipper for even distribution of water.

300. Pressing Blankets.

Press only the binding of blankets; ironing ruins the nap, which is the warmth-giving quality of a blanket.

301. Crease Out of Hems.

To lower hems, use slightly diluted clear white vinegar to steam out the old hemline. It really works!

302. Press With Paper.

Don't give away that too-short dress of permanent press material. The crease of the old hem can be removed by pressing with strips of wet brown paper. To extend the hem for sewing, add wide lace used for facing.

303. Ironing Linen.

Avoid ironing creases in your linen napkins and tablecloths in the same place each time. It will break the threads and cause wear in the linen.

304. Ironing Aid.

A dampened cellulose sponge will provide just the necessary amount of water to dampen dry spots on a garment when ironing.

305. Use a bit of bluing to tint the starch you use on dark blue or black materials to keep it from showing white on the cloth.

306. Dirty Clothespin Marks.

Marks left on your clean laundry by dirty clothespins need not happen again if you bleach the pins. Soak them in a pan containing half a cup of household bleach. Then rinse well and dry thoroughly.

307. Prevent Color From Running.

A tablespoon of black pepper added to the first suds in which you are washing cottons will keep colors from running.

308. To Soften Hard Water. . .

add a teaspoon of washing soda to each gallon of water.

309. Care of Lace on Nylon.

Since nylon is not starched, it is a problem to keep cotton lace crisp on a nylon blouse. Solve this by placing waxed paper under the lace, then pressing with a warm iron.

310. Lint-Free Bath Towels.

If lint gets on dark-colored bath towels, rinse the towels separately through two waters. Add vinegar—a tablespoon to a gallon of water—for the third rinse. When dry, towels will be fluffy and lint-free, and will have no vinegar odor.

311. Body to Curtains.

Did you know that ½ cup of milk powder added to the last rinsing water will restore "body" to nylon or dacron curtains?

312. Care of Nylons.

After washing nylon stockings, rinse them in water containing several tablespoons of vinegar. This will make the nylon more flexible and less apt to run.

313. Small magnets hold nylon articles to a shower rod, and the garments will dry faster.

314. Remove Perspiration Stains

on washable apparel by applying a thick paste of baking soda to the stain and leave it on 15 minutes.

315. Soaking Clothes.

Don't let the hot water get cold that you soak your clothes in. This can cause the fabric to hold dirt.

316. Lemon Juice to Renew Yellowed Lace.

If a piece of lace or embroidery has become yellowed with age, it may be bleached to look new again by boiling it in water to which lemon juice has been added.

317. Washing Mop Head.

Put a soiled mop head into a worn nylon stocking, knot both top and foot, then let the bundle spin in the washer with hot suds. The mop comes out clean, and the stocking prevents its lint from spreading.

318. Use of Old Umbrella.

If you have an old umbrella, remove the fabric and hang the frame upside down for a handy place to dry diapers, tea towels, dishcloths, etc.

319. Washing Woolens.

Woolens should never be washed in hot water; use lukewarm water and plenty of suds. Don't soak. If washed in a machine, three minutes washing time is sufficient. Rinse thoroughly in lukewarm water; squeeze, do not twist. Dry on a flat surface.

320. Use of Bluing.

A little bluing added to the water along with the soap makes white clothes whiter and colored pieces brighter.

321. White Collars and Cuffs.

Dip a discarded tooth-brush in a bleach solution and rub white collars and cuffs of colored dresses before laundering. Keeps them sparkling white.

322. Rubber Sheets.

To keep baby's rubber sheet smelling fresh, add a few drops of cologne to the rinse water when you wash it.

323. Grease Spots on Cotton.

Grease spots on solid color cottons are hard to remove with ordinary soap and water. Wet each spot with Mufti before laundering for better results.

324. To Soften Wool. . .

add one teaspoon of borax to a gallon of lukewarm water for rinsing woolens.

325. Proper Sorting.

Proper sorting of laundry is half the battle. Clothes should be sorted according to color, and also according to how soiled they are. Then the very soiled pieces can get extra soap or bleach and more washing time.

326. Preparation.

Remove pins and buckles, turn pockets inside out, turn down cuffs, get rid of grass or sand. Check for stains which should be treated first.

327. Water Softener.

Soft water gives better results. If the water is hard, buy a good commercial water softener.

328. Short Soaking Period.

Soaking clothes overnight tends to give them a grayish appearance. A fifteen-minute period in cool water gets better results.

329. Laundering Tufted Bedspreads.

When laundering tufted bedspreads in the washing machine, place them in a pillow case, and thus protect the tufting.

330. All Gone.

Stains don't stand a chance against this treatment, which is especially good for getting rid of stains on baby things: Mix ¼ cup chlorine bleach with ½ cup automatic dishwasher detergent and 1 gallon *hot* water. Soak clothes 30 minutes, then wash as usual. Use this method *only* for clothing that is chlorine-bleach safe.

SHORT CUTS
To Good
House
Cleaning

331. Turn an ordinary scrub brush into a handier brush by fastening a discarded wooden drawer knob to the wooden back of the scrub brush with a screw.

332. Tip Cover for Mop and Broom.

Cover broom and mop handles at their tips with fingers from old rubber gloves. This keeps them from slipping and sliding when placed against a wall.

333. Between Waxings.

Use cold water and a little vinegar to mop linoleum floors between waxings. Dirt and grease will be removed, but the wax will remain on the floors.

334. To Take Away Furniture Scratches.

To make most furniture scratches disappear, take one-half a walnut meat, break it in two and rub its inner surface gently over the scratch. Touch up scratches on mahogany with iodine; on ebony with black shoe polish.

335. Piano Care.

Sudden temperature changes injure the tune of a piano. Keep away from radiators or windows.

336. To Clean Piano Keys . . .

dampen a cloth in denatured alcohol. Never use soap, for it stains ivory keys.

337. Play Your Piano . . .

at least a few hours each week to keep it in good playing condition.

338. Paint Metal Salt Shaker Tops . . .

with clear fingernail polish to prevent rusting. When dry, punch out the holes with a large needle.

339. Copper Cleaner.

Make an economical cleaner for copper: use half a lemon dipped in salt. Rub vigorously and rinse with hot water and polish with a dry cloth.

340. Cleaning Leather Chairs.

Clean your leather chairs with saddle soap.

341. Rug Cleaner.

Slightly soiled rugs may be cleaned with corn meal. Sprinkle on and rub in with a stiff brush. Remove with the vacuum cleaner.

342. Floor Protection.

Wax the rockers and feet of chairs and furniture every time you wax the floor to prevent scratches on the floor.

343. Upholstered Furniture.

Frequent cleaning of upholstered furniture with the vacuum or a brush is a good moth preventive measure. Clean thoroughly and often.

344. Patching Upholstery.

A piece of adhesive tape makes a fine patch for torn upholstery. Place the tape on the bottom side and draw the torn edges together smoothly.

345. Long Life for Mattresses.

To prolong the life of a mattress make a dust-proof cover of heavy muslin and use a quilted pad.

346. Mattress Cleaning.

An innerspring mattress should be turned over once a week, and cleaned thoroughly with the vacuum.

347. More Mattress Care.

Never sit on the edge of a mattress. Never stand them on end or beat.

348. Cleaning in Corners.

Use a small paint brush to dust out corners of chairs or to get at recessed areas in heavy carved furniture.

349. First, Warm Furniture Polish.

You can do a quicker polishing job if you first warm the furniture polish in hot water before you begin applying it to furniture. Warm furniture polish penetrates wood pores faster than cold polish.

350. Car Wax. . .

is good for polishing wood also. It gives good protection and a low gloss shine.

351. Spray-on Starch for Busy Doors.

For a much-used door that collects fingerprints too often, spray with spray-on starch in the most used areas. This will keep the door clean and glossy and free from fingerprints.

352. Windowsill Protection.

Wax the windowsills to protect them from rain and soot. Waxing at least every 2 or 3 months and dusting every day will keep them in good condition without any hard cleaning on your part.

353. Drying Boots.

Take a discarded dish rack and set it in a foil-lined box. The family footwear can drip dry in the box without making a mess which requires cleaning later. Place the box on the porch or in the front hall where it can accommodate all the wet rubbers and overshoes.

354. Make a Cleaning Basket. . .

of a small open market basket; assemble brushes, dusters, cleansers, polish, etc., to be carried easily from room to room.

355. Make Your Own Deodorizer. . .

by mixing a little household ammonia in a bowl of water; leave in a room overnight to remove tobacco and other stale odors.

356. Remove White Spots on Mahogany. . .

by spreading a coat of vaseline on the spot for 48 hours.

357. Vinegar for Lots of Uses.

An ordinary cloth dampened with a little vinegar takes the place of lots of one-job cleaners all around the house. A quick rub makes spotty stainless steel bright and shiny again, puts luster back in cloudy varnished wood surfaces, cleans stained vases and fishbowls crystal clear.

358. Make a Good Polishing Mitt

by using old clean socks. Have one dampened with polish and one dry. Work with both hands and finish in half the time.

359. Felt Pads for Furniture.

Cut rounds of old felt hats and glue to the feet of all furniture to save scratching polished floors.

360. Homemade Furniture Polish.

To 1 quart of hot water add 3 tablespoons linseed oil and 1 tablespoon turpentine. Mix well and cool. Wring a soft cloth out of this solution, and apply to furniture. Dry at once and polish.

361. To Brighten Mirrors. . .

rub well with a cloth dampened in alcohol.

or

362. To Make Mirrors Sparkle. . .

add a little bluing to the water used to clean them.

363. Remove Paint Splashes from Windows.

Use turpentine or hot vinegar to loosen paint splashes from windows. The use of a razor blade scratches the glass.

364. Lustre for Hearth Tiles.

Wax your hearth tiles for added lustre, after washing and thoroughly drying.

365. Window-Washing Solution.

Mix your own window washing solution, two tablespoons of household ammonia added to two quarts of warm water is perfect for washing mirrors and windows.

366. To Remove Old Wax. . .

from your floors, use turpentine, then wash thoroughly with warm water and soap before rewaxing.

367. Use No Abrasives on Linoleum. . .

only mild soap and warm water to prolong the life of the linoleum. To remove old wax, add a package of water softener and cleaner to the warm suds when washing.

368. Polish for Antiques. . .

can be made with two parts turpentine and one part linseed oil. Apply with a soft cloth, rub off and polish with a dry cloth.

369. Waxing With a Paint Roller.

Waxing floors can be made easier by applying the wax with a paint roller attached to a broom handle.

370. Liquid Starch for Linoleum.

Add several tablespoons of liquid starch to the warm soapsuds you use to scrub the linoleum floors. This will keep the floor glistening.

371. A Cotton Swab. . .

makes a good little paint brush for filling in a nick.

372. For More Room. . .

in the linen closet, try standing sheets up like books on a shelf.

373. A Dingy-Looking Lampshade. . .

can sometimes be revived by coating it with a thick paste of starch, letting it dry, and later brushing off.

374. Cleaning Lamp Shades.

Silk and rayon lamp shades may be washed if they are hand stitched. Never wash a lamp shade that is glued to the frame. Stitched shades can be washed in a rich soap suds with a small brush. Rinse thoroughly, pat with a soft towel, and dry in the shade.

375. Soap Saver.

Place small pieces of cellulose sponge in all soap dishes for economy. They will keep the soap firm and dry but will retain enough soap to be handy for washing the sink or lavatory.

376. Cleaning Cloths.

If cleaning cloths are hemmed and washed out before they become too soiled, they can be used again and again.

377. Shake Your Dust Mop in a Bag.

Never shake the dust mop out the window and scatter the dust. Tie a paper bag around the mop head and shake well, dispose of the bag and dust.

378. Cleaning Wicker Furniture.

Scrub wicker furniture with a good stiff brush and warm salt water. Salt keeps the wicker from turning yellow.

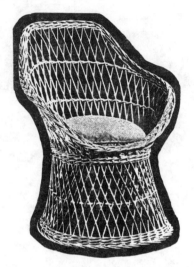

379. Protection From Ashes.

When removing ashes from the fireplace, burn a newspaper in one corner, and the dust will be drawn up the chimney instead of into the room.

380. New Life for Brooms.

A broom should be washed at intervals in warm water to which a little household ammonia has been added. Rinse in clear water and hang up to dry.

381. Salty Broom.

Dip a new broom in hot salt water before using. Use a half-cup of salt to a gallon of water. It will toughen the bristles and give your broom added life.

382. Venetian Blind Dusters.

One of the best dusters for Venetian blinds is a pair of cotton gloves turned inside out. Slip on a pair and go over the blinds; when soiled change to a clean pair. Come washday, drop them in the washing machine.

383. Rubber Sponge for Bathroom.

Keep a small rubber sponge in your bathroom for cleaning the lavatory and wiping up spots on the floor, and do away with unsightly rags.

384. Suction Cups for Towel Racks.

To avoid driving nails in your plastered walls, use rubber suction cups for mounting towel racks, etc. They can then be mounted to the side of the refrigerator or a piece of furniture.

385. Prevent Sticking Dresser Drawers.

When the furnace is going and the woodwork is thoroughly dry is the time to apply a good coat of paste wax to the tops of doors and the edges of drawers. The wax will close the pores of the wood and prevent swelling and sticking on damp days next summer.

386. Comforters and Their Care.

Roll slippery satin comforters and insert in a pillow case. Then they will stack with other blankets and stay dust-free.

China and Silverware Care

387. Add Milk to Brighten Silverware.

Try adding a little milk to the water in which you wash your silverware. The milk will keep the silverware bright.

388. Keep Silver From Tarnishing.

Add a little piece of gum camphor to a drawer filled with silverware to keep silver from tarnishing for some time.

389.
If your silverware becomes tarnished, take out a clean aluminum pan, dissolve in it a teaspoonful of table salt and a teaspoon ful of baking soda to each quart of boiling water. Immerse the silverware until tarnish is removed; then rinse in a clean warm water and rub dry with a clean, soft cloth.

390. Wrapping Silver.

Plastic wrap placed around silver teapots, candlesticks, and tableware keeps them from tarnishing.

391. Silver Polisher.

Paper napkins are fine for polishing silver.

392.
Use an old shaving brush to dust fragile china bric-a-brac.

393. Storing China.

When storing good china, put paper doilies between each plate and saucer to prevent scratching.

394. China Crack Filler.

Put that cracked dish in a pan of milk and boil forty-five minutes. The crack will disappear.

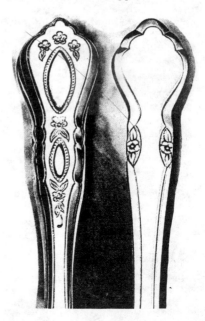

PERSONAL GROOMING

395. Make a Plan.

Have a plan for your entire wardrobe before you make a single purchase; then you can make the most of the accessories you have on hand.

396. Look "Like a Million."

Care for your clothing is important. Careful darning, level hemlines, all buttons and snaps in place, spotlessly clean keep you looking "like a million."

397. Soft Hair Curlers.

If your small daughter has very thin hair, try rolling it on pipe cleaners; they make soft curls and will not split the ends of her hair.

398. Holder for Lingerie Straps.

To prevent slip and brassiere straps from sliding off your shoulders, sew the back side of a safety pin to the shoulder seams of your dress about an inch from the neckline. Slip straps through the pin and close it. Straps will not fall off, and will slide back and forth easily as you move.

399. Clean Costume Jewelry.

One way to clean costume jewelry is to wipe it with a soft cloth that has been dipped in rubbing alcohol.

400. Touchup Makeup!

Ladies, when makeup shows travel stain, a witch hazel pad will smooth the streaks and refresh the face at the same time.

401. Unmanageable Hair.

For hair that can't keep a set, try a package of unflavored gelatin with barely warm water as an after shampoo rinse.

402. Refrigerator Nail Polish.

Fingernail polish will stay "good to the last drop" if you'll keep it in the refrigerator.

403. To Remove Ring From Swollen Finger. . .

grease the finger with petroleum jelly. If the ring does not slide off, soak the hand in ice-cold soapsuds.

404. Restringing Beads.

If you restring beads, dip the end of the thread in glue and allow this tip to dry, forming a sturdy needle substitute. Nylon thread and dental floss may be used to restring beads. These products are strong and durable.

405. Facial Tissues for Lipstick.

Keep a box of facial tissues in the bathroom, fine for removing lipstick and cold cream, saves towels.

406. Restful Foot Bath.

A half cup of salt in a basin of hot water makes a wonderful footbath.

407. Clean Rhinestone Jewelry.

Soak rhinestone jewelry in gasoline about 15 minutes, then rub with a flannel cloth.

408. Use Powder Puff to Apply Polish.

An old powder puff from a compact is fine for applying white shoe polish. Wash and see how well it works. Your fingers will not be soiled as the polish does not penetrate the puff. Rinse it out and dry it and it is ready for use the next time.

409. To Seal Perfume

take a few drops of candle wax to seal your perfume when traveling. Then take the candle with you to seal the perfume for the return trip.

410. Plagued With Dry Skin?

If you are plagued with dry skin, there's a way to cleanse it without using soap and water. That creamy baby lotion that softens skins is also an excellent cleanser. The lotion contains oils that help dissolve soil and makeup, and it also contains water to wash it away. Apply the lotion over your face; then wipe off with cotton puffs.

411. Perfume for Hankies.

Perfume your handkerchiefs with a little orris root tied in a muslin bag, used in the water in which you launder them.

412. To Clean Brushes and Combs. . .

put them in a jar containing about a quart of water and one-fourth cup of ammonia.

413. Mineral Oil Protects Hands.

Apply a few drops of mineral oil to your hands before starting work, and it will protect your skin as efficiently as rubber gloves, and without hampering your movements.

414. To prevent container openings from sticking, particularly on nail-polish bottles, tubes of glue, cans of varnish, nonaerosol hair spray, etc., rub petroleum jelly inside the cover and on the grooves before using for the first time.

Removing
STAINS

415. Baked-on Stains. . .

can be softened by placing a shallow dish of ammonia in the closed oven overnight.

416. Lime Deposits. . .

may be removed from glass bottles or pitchers by filling them with suds and about two tablespoons of vinegar. Let them soak, swish the suds around, then rinse and dry.

417. Clean Hands. . .

quickly with a piece of cut lemon. Rub it over the hands and rinse with clear water. The lemon juice will remove stains and grime and help to keep hands looking nice always.

418. Remove Ballpoint Pen Ink

from fingers by rubbing with a cloth dampened with milk.

419. To remove grease from wood paneling, scrub with a cloth saturated with lacquer thinner.

420. A great stain may often be removed from wallpaper by applying liquid starch from a push-button container to the spot and letting it dry. When the starch is dry, wipe it off with a clean cloth. If the stain isn't fully gone, repeat the treatment.

421. Use lemon juice or vinegar to remove from porcelain rust stains caused by leaking faucets.

422. Baking Soda for Perspiration Stains.

Use baking soda paste to remove perspiration stains from white blouses and shirts. Use one heaping tablespoon of soda in cup of warm water. When you do shirts, squeeze just the underarm parts in this water; when thoroughly wet, let stand 20 minutes before laundering.

423. Whitening Hankies.

Discolored handkerchiefs may be whitened by soaking them in cold water to which a pinch of cream of tartar has been added.

424. Baby Oil on Chrome.

Use baby oil to remove stains from the chrome trim on kitchen appliances. Just apply a small amount with a soft cloth, then polish.

425. Tea Stains.

To make stubborn tea stains vanish in a cup, rub the sides briskly with salt.

426. Soiled Necklines.

Powder and makeup can be cleaned from collars by dipping a soft cloth in vinegar and applying to soiled necklines.

427. Bathtub Stain.

Stains on a sink or bathtub can be removed with a paste made of hydrogen peroxide and cream of tartar.

428. White Shoe Polish for Crochet.

If you get a small spot on white crocheted table mats, dab it with white shoe polish, and you can use it many times before laundering and restarching.

429. Tile Bleach.

Make a powder of household bleach and a cleansing powder, apply to tile in the kitchen and bath, let stand fifteen minutes, rinse off to remove stains.

430. Cod Liver Oil. . .

stains can be removed by dipping in gasoline, then sponge with warm suds.

431. Orange Juice. . .

stains can be removed by sprinkling baking soda on both sides of the stain, moisten with water, and let stand a few minutes.

432. Lipstick.

Loosen with vaseline or glycerin and launder as usual.

433. Ink.

Soak in cold water, then apply lemon juice or vinegar.

434. Mildew.

Wash in hot suds, moisten with lemon juice and salt, dry in sun.

435. Nail Polish.

Use polish remover, sponge remaining stain with denatured alcohol.

436. Chewing Gum.

Rub with a piece of ice, and scrape.

437. Automobile Grease.

If washable material, rub lard into the spot, leave overnight, and launder.

438. To Remove Finger Marks from Felt Hats. . .

rub with very fine sandpaper.

439. Fruit Stains.

Pour boiling water through the stain. If stain remains use hydrogen peroxide.

440. Tobacco.

Wash with warm water, then sponge with lemon juice or chlorine bleach.

441. Water Spots on Velvet.

Remove by holding over steam from a teakettle for a few minutes. When completely dry, brush with a piece of velvet.

442. Gravy. . .

can be ironed out between two blotters.

443. Adhesive Tape Marks. . .

will come off easily if rubbed with a little alcohol.

444. Non-Washable Materials.

Should be taken to a reliable drycleaner, since special cleaning agents are required.

445. To Remove Ballpoint Ink Stain. . .

from material, dab on concentrated hair shampoo or spray on hair spray, rub out the ink, then launder the item as usual.

CHILDREN
in the HOME

446. Rubber Pad on Swing Seat.

A rubber pad placed on the seat of a child's swing keeps small fry from falling off and also protects from injury by splinters.

447. Substitute Bluing for Ink.

Most children yearn to write with ink. Let them use liquid bluing instead. In case it spills on clothes or table, bluing will wash out easily.

448. Protect Heels With Tacks.

If the children's heels wear down too quickly, hammer a couple of small carpet tacks into the heel where most of the wear occurs.

449. Feed Food From Bottle.

When an infant is ill and fussy, he would rather not eat his food; but I have discovered that when he will not eat from a spoon, he will usually take his food from a bottle if you enlarge the opening in the nipple. The food will flow easily, and the baby will get his nourishment.— Mrs. Paul Crossman, Jr.

450. Cleaning Child's Sneakers.

Use a moistened, soapy scouring pad to clean the white rubber on your child's sneakers. For extra-heavy soil or tar marks, use a scouring powder.

451. Easy-to-Zip Fastener.

Slip a small key chain through the hole in the tab of the slide fastener to make it easy to zip a child's jacket. This provides something for the youngster to grip and makes it easier for the child to get his jacket on and off.

452. Use of Discarded Card Table.

Save that discarded old card table, cut the legs down, and repair it enough so that it can be used for a child's table. Then take it along on picnics, and the little folks will have a table to eat on, as it is harder for them to balance plates and cups or sit at the higher tables.

453. How to Keep a Child's Attention.

A sure method of gaining and keeping a child's attention while reading stories is to substitute his name for that of the hero of the story.

454. Rubber Jar Rings. . .

make an excellent and easy-to-hold toy for babies just learning to hold objects.

455. Easy to Identify.

Snapshots of your children pasted on their books and lunch boxes will save a lot of quarreling over ownership.

456. Powder Diapers Before Folding.

Save time by sprinkling powder on your baby's diapers when you fold them. This way the baby will be sure to get some powder at every change.

457. Hold Slippery Glass With Cotton Sock.

Babies sometimes have trouble holding on to a glass of milk. Cover that slippery glass with a cotton sock. If the bottle should drop and break, the pieces of glass will remain inside the sock.

458. Patching Snowsuits.

When patching the knees of children's snowsuits, place patches of vinyl plastic under the regular patches. Stitch both together on the pants. These make long-lasting, waterproof patches.

459. Long Life for Crib Sheets.

To prolong the life of a crib sheet and amuse the child, patch the worn spots with cut out animals from printed cotton materials. Trace the animals from his color book.

460. Fitted Sheets.

To make a snug-fitting sheet for a child's plastic covered mattress, sew together two sheets like a pillow case the exact size of the mattress. To change sheets just turn the mattress.

461. Rubber Pad for Junior's Wagon.

You can save your youngster painful bruises and save on darning trousers, too, if you put a pad of rubber sponge in the bed of his wagon, to kneel on.

462. Wax Wooden Toys.

If children's wooden toys have a good coat of paste wax when they are new, it is easy to keep dust and dirt from getting into the wood; then they can be wiped off with a damp cloth.

463. Footstool for Beginners.

Place a sturdy footstool near the sink if your four year old is learning to dry dishes. Added height will give her confidence and cut down on breakage.

464. Hang a Low Mirror for Children.

Small children will take a keen interest in washing their faces and brushing their teeth if a mirror is hung low enough for them to see themselves.

465. Make a Bandage Secure.

To prevent a bandage slipping off a small child's hand, cut off the fingertips of an old clean white glove, and slip over the bandage.

466. Container for Toys.

A set of kitchen canisters decorated with nursery decals are fine for storing children's small toys, marbles and crayons.

or

A gay-colored lightweight plastic dishpan or bucket will make a wonderful storage place for a youngster's toys. Either will be light enough for the toddler to manage.

467. Crayon Remover.

When small children write on the wallpaper with wax crayons, it can be removed by rubbing lightly with very fine steel wool, with no damage to the paper.

468. Ice cream cones are grand gelatin dessert cups for children's parties.

469. If you put cold cream on the forehead of children, soap will not run in their eyes when washing hair.

GIFT and
PARTY
Suggestions

470. It's Fun to Entertain. . .

once you've broken the ice. Collect a group of friends and have a party. Let the children help. It will give dignity to your home, and help your children develop poise.

471. Who to Invite.

Be sure the group you invite mix well.

472. Choose Your Type of Entertaining.

Whether it be the next door neighbor, the Boy Scout troop, the new couple down the street, your husband's boss, or "Aunt Minnie," discover the easiest type of entertaining for your household.

473. Plan a Menu with Which You Are Familiar.

Never try out new dishes for the first time when you are entertaining. Choose one that can be prepared well before dinnertime. Casserole dishes are a wonderful solution.

474. Serve an Appetizer.

A first course of chilled juice may be served in the living room.

475. Simplify Serving.

Make a big bowl of mixed salad to be served at the table. Make a dessert that can also be served at the table.

476. Put Your House in Order.

Have your house sweet and clean. Add fresh flowers or leaves. Do most of the work the day before, so you won't be too tired.

477. Keep Holidays.

Celebrate holidays; they help bring the family together, and offer wonderful excuses for parties.

478. Permanent "Fixings."

For each important holiday acquire some special mantle and table decorations; keep stored in labeled boxes. They give a festive air to holidays.

479. Give an Exchange Party.

Ask each guest to bring a group of unwanted but usable articles to trade. The articles may exchange ownership several times before the party is over; it makes a friendly get-together for neighbors.

480. Make Your Own Place Cards

for a luncheon or dinner with fresh flowers from your own garden. Use small linen cards with a tiny rosebud or any small flower; tie in the corner with ribbon, and print the name with the same color of ink as the flower.

481. Attractive Package for Birthday.

Make an attractive package for a child's birthday; if she is six, glue six bright pennies to the ribbon with which the gift is tied.

482. Add a Toy.

If you are giving clothing, please a little child by adding a dimestore toy in the pocket.

483. Cookie Carrier.

When your gift is cookies or a cake, put it in a paper plate lined with paper doily. It looks attractive and spares the obligation of returning a plate.

487. Paint Remover.

To remove fresh or old paint from cloth, soak the spots in equal parts of turpentine and ammonia for two hours, then wash.

488. Paint Brush Cleaner.

Stiff paint brushes can be made pliable if soaked in hot vinegar.

489. Before storing paint, mark a line with it on the outside of the can to indicate its level. Then you can tell at a glance how much is left and what color it is.

OUTSIDE
Jobs—Activities

484. Clean Paint Brushes. . .

by placing them in a container filled with plain cooking oil. The paint comes out with the oil when washed, and there's no evaporation or odor as there is with turpentine.

485. Storing Paint, Varnish, etc.

Store cans of paint, varnish, thinner, or other inflammables and oil rags in sturdy galvanised cans with tight-fitting lids. Then set the cans in the garage until you are ready to use them again.

486. Drop Cloth.

An old plastic tablecloth or draperies make fine drop cloths when there is painting to be done.

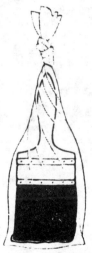

490. To keep a paintbrush or roller from drying out, slip it into a plastic bag, twist to remove air, and knot.

491. A Varnish Tip.

Set your can of varnish in a pan of very hot water while using, and it will brush on a surface more smoothly.

492. Paint Preserver.

A part of a can of paint will not harden if sealed airtight. Before storing turn the can upside down for a moment, until enough paint flows around the edges to seal and make it airtight, then turn right side up and store.

493. To Keep Loose Grass and Dirt out of the House. . .

tack a small scrub brush, bristle side up, in a convenient but inconspicuous place near the back door and use it to wipe off shoes before entering the house.

494. Handy Auto Brush.

Trim an old whisk broom down to a point, and make a handy brush for cleaning automobile seats, etc.

495. Slip-Proof Ladders.

Give your ladder a slip-proof treatment, apply shellac to the steps; while still wet, sprinkle with coarse sand or sawdust, let harden. Good for basement steps, also.

496. Repair. . .

small leaks in hose with a generous application of black rubber-base cement.

497. Wasp Nest.

To get rid of a wasp nest put gasoline in a spray bottle and spray on nest.

498. Keep Bird Bath from Freezing. . .

by adding a few drops of glycerin to the bird bath in cold weather.

499. Candle Stubs for Lighting Fires.

Save candle stubs for lighting fires. One small piece of candle will start a fire even when the kindling is wet.

500. Insect Repellent.

Moth crystals sprinkled in the garbage can in hot weather will keep insects away.

501. Wax Paper for Sticky Paint.

To prevent shelf paper from sticking to freshly painted shelves, use wax paper first; it will not stick.

502. Rust Remover for Chrome.

No need to buy expensive rust removers for your car's chrome. Try aluminum foil. Just roll it up into a ball, dampen it with water, and rub the area.

503. Sulphur Vs. Red Ants.

Try powdered sulphur for red ants. It will solve the problem and is perfectly harmless. It can also be used outside around the foundation or around fruit trees. The ants won't come near the sulphur.

504.

When setting out tomato plants, put a nail close to the plant; the cutworms will not eat them off.

Take the
CHILDREN
With
You

505. Vacations Can Be Fun.

Places take on a new interest when seen through the eyes of young children. You can have fun and get to know your children while they get to know the world.

506. Out of Season Vacations.

It costs less to travel in winter; vacation prices are lower, and crowds are smaller.

507. Make a Plan.

It takes a little planning to keep children comfortable and amused. Be sure to take a simple first aid kit. There's nothing like a good-looking bandage to soothe a child.

508. Entertainment Enroute.

A bag filled with small toys, each wrapped separately, one to be opened each day, will work a miracle. Cut-out books and blunt scissors, story books and crayons are a must for children.

509. Make a Check List.

Start a list well in advance. Add to it as you think of things to take. Be sure to include addresses of folks you should write to while away.

510. Packing Jewelry.

The next time you pack a suitcase, put your jewelry and other fragile items in a pair of socks and stick them into your shoes.

511. Take Along Clothespins.

Pack a few clip-on clothespins in your suitcase. They will quickly turn a wire hanger into a skirt or pants holder.

512. Good Use for Road Map.

Wrap a going-away present in a road map. You will be giving the recipient two gifts in one.

513. Portable Snack Bar.

Car travel calls for emergency

rations. A few boxes of cookies, some fruit juices, crackers, favorite canned meat, fruit and jelly for a picnic on the way. By all means take a thermos of ice water.

514. Remember to—

Lock all windows; ask the paper boy and milk man to stop service.

515. On Vacation—

Use jelly glasses for drinking glasses. Initial each with colored nail polish. When every child has his own glass you save on dishwashing.

516. Take Your Corn Popper.

Be sure to take your corn popper on an auto trip. It can be used for heating soup, making instant coffee or boiling water for baby's formula.

517. Tie Baby's Toys to the Car.

Tie the baby's beads and toys with lengths of ribbon to the door handles, so he can enjoy them without throwing them out the window.

518. To Spot Your Car.

To locate your car in a large parking area, tie a handkerchief or scarf to the radio aerial and push it up as far as it will go when you park. You can spot your car many blocks away.

FLOWERS and
GARDENING

519. Start Some Bulbs.

Watching a real flower emerge from a bulb in the spring is a wonderful and rewarding way to teach a young child some of the wonder of Nature. Let your child start a few bulbs in the fall and watch them grow.

520. Unusual Plant.

The top of a fresh pineapple, planted in a pint container of water, will sprout and root, making an unusual house plant.

521. New Life for Wax Flowers.

Dip wax flowers in alcohol and wipe gently with a soft paint brush.

522. Hanging Vine.

A beautiful hanging vine can be grown from a sweet potato. Plant in a pot of sand, keep well watered; or they may be grown in water only.

523. Treatment for Fresh Flowers.

To keep cut flowers fresh, place in deep cold water for a few hours before arranging, Cut the stems on a long slant, and remove all foliage below the water.

524. Prolong Life of Cut Flowers. . .

by adding a lump of sugar or camphor to the water.

525. Fresh Air for Flowers.

Flowers thrive on fresh air. Keep fresh air in the room; avoid direct heat and drafts.

526. Simple Aid for Plants.

Put several empty egg shells in a bottle filled with water; let stand for 24 hours and water plants with it. A good treatment for house plants.

527. Waterproof a Clay Flower Pot. . .

by simply dipping it in melted paraffin.

528. Garden Tools.

Paint the handles of garden tools with bright orange paint; it will protect the wood, and make them easy to find.

529. Mailing "Cuttings."

A good container in which to mail "cuttings" can be made from a milk carton. Put a small amount of damp soil in the bottom and insert the cutting. Pack tissue around the foliage and wrap for mailing.

530. How to Water Indoor Plants.

Use a meat baster to water your indoor plants and African violets. This way you can use just the right amount, and you won't get water on the leaves of delicate plants.

531. To Save Choice Seed. . .

from a choice blossom, tie a small paper bag over the blossom before the seeds are ripe enough to scatter. As the seeds ripen they will drop into the bag.

532. Foliage Plants Make Better House Plants. . .

than flowering ones; they do not require as much sunshine, and can take warmth better.

533. Rooting Potted Plants.

When a cutting from a potted plant is hard to root, cover it with a clear drinking glass until it takes root.

534. Save That Last Bloom.

Don't discard flowers when they begin to fade; pick off withered blooms, cut down the stalk and rearrange in a smaller container; make your cut flowers last twice as long.

535. Place a charcoal tablet in the water that holds a floral arrangement. It will help to keep the water pure.

536. Protect Hose from Sun.

Number one enemy of your garden hose is exposure to sunlight.

537. Protection from Heavy Traffic.

You can ruin the best hose by running over it with the wheelbarrow or auto.

538. Use a Rack for Storing.

Never hang a hose on a nail; use a rack or reel for storing.

539. Dust Those Plants!

Household plants must be dusted and washed because a layer of dust on plant leaves will deprive the plant of necessary light.

540. A Container for Flowers.

Cover an inverted cheese carton with colorful foil and use it as a container for artificial flowers. Punch holes in the bottom of the container and insert your artificial flower stems.

541. Before Filling Flower Pots With Dirt. . .

cut out a piece of old cloth to fit the bottom of the pot. Dampen the cloth and place it inside the pot so that it covers the drain holes. The cloth will not prevent drainage, but it will prevent the seepage of dirt particles through the drain holes.

542. Paraffin for Flower Pots.

Dip the edges of clay pots in melted paraffin before planting African violets and other house plants, and when the leaves touch the pot they will not wither and die.

543. Keeping Onions Fresh.

To avoid wasting unused spring onions, replant in the flower bed until needed. They will continue to grow and stay fresh until the last one is used.

544. Sponge Soaks Up Moisture.

A piece of moistened sponge placed in the bottom of a flower pot will help retain moisture and cut down the time spent in watering the plant.

545. Unflavored Gelatin for House Plants.

Knox Unflavored Gelatin has lots of nitrogen—just what houseplants need most. Mix 1 envelope with 1 cup of hot tap water to dissolve. Then slowly add 3 cups of cold water. Once a month use this mixture as part of your normal watering pattern. Make up just enough mixture for one time.

PET CARE

546. Suction Cup Holds Dish.

Attach a rubber suction cup to the bottom of your pet's feeding dish so that the dish will not slide on the floor while the pet is eating.

547. Removing Pet Hair.

If you have a pet in your home, dog or cat hairs are bound to be on your upholstered furniture. You can remove these hairs by rubbing the furniture lightly with a damp rubber sponge.

548. Watering Pan for Pets.

Make an outside watering pan for pets or chickens with an angel-food cake pan. Drive a stake firmly into the ground through the stem of the pan. Can't turn over.

549. Vacuum the Cat.

The upholstery attachment of the vacuum can be used to remove loose hair from your Persian cat. Run it lightly over the entire body, except ears, and catch that loose hair before the sofa catches it.

550. Soda Controls Litter Pan Odor.

Dump a pound box of baking soda into the bottom of a litter pan, spread around so soda covers the bottom. Then use the empty box as a measure and add three boxes of litter. You have a quick, economical recipe for controlling litter pan odors.

551. Housebreaking Fido.

Try this trick for housebreaking a puppy: Hang a bell by a rubber band—so that it bounces—from a doorknob. Each time the puppy is taken outside to "perform," ring the bell. Within a few days he will be able to tell *you* when he needs to go out.

552. Keeping Fleas off Fido.

The arrival of spring means that flea season is just around the corner. Begin protecting your canines early...by sprinkling powdered brewer's yeast over their daily rations. One tablespoon daily dose for large dogs (try giving one *teaspoon* to small breeds) will—if continued throughout the season—discourage the insects from taking up residence on your four-legged friends.

Puppy bathtime

553. Fill a tub with warm water and put a rubber mat on the bottom for secure footing.

554. Put cotton in your dog's ears to keep out water and a little petroleum jelly around his eyes to protect them from soap.

555. Add a little baking soda to rinse water to make your pet's coat softer, shinier and odor-free.

556. Baking soda or dry cornmeal is a good dry shampoo for any furry pet. Rub it in well, then brush it out.

557. "Canned" Dog Food.

Store big bags of dry dog food in a clean garbage can with a lid.

558. Finicky Felines.

Your cat won't be so choosy if some oil from a can of tuna is sprinkled over his food.

559. Cheaper Cat-Litter Liners.

A box of ten plastic lawn bags makes forty litter-pan liners. Cut each bag into four large rectangular pieces.

OTHER

HELPFUL

HINTS

Taming of the Screw.

Keep a bolt tight simply by putting a second nut on the bolt and tightening it against the first nut.

Dishwasher.

The washing cycle of your dishwasher actually uses much less hot water than washing dishes by hand. It's the drying cycle that eats up so much electricity. So when the wash cycle is completed, open the door and let the dishes air dry.

That's Real Coffee.

To revive scratched and dull wooden platters and bowls—especially dark woods—make a thick paste of instant coffee and water for a nontoxic stain. Rub in the stain with a clean sponge or cloth; wipe off any excess.

Sit Tight.

Are your small ones forever slipping and slouching in their high chairs? Apply textured bathtub appliques to the seat and back of the high chair. No more slide-away baby!

The Chill Is Off.

Cold body lotion after a nice warm tub or shower gives me the shivers. If I take a plastic bottle of lotion into the shower with me, the chill is off by the time I'm ready to slather it on.

Rub-A-Dub-Dub.

Dirty oven racks can be cleaned easily in the bathtub. First, place a bath towel in the tub to prevent scratches. Then add 1 cup automatic dishwasher detergent and ½ cup vinegar to a tubful of hot water. Soak at least one hour. The burned-on food will slip right off. If any remains, it can be scrubbed off easily. Finally, rinse and dry and replace racks in oven.

Something Fishy.

When you change the water in your fresh-water aquarium, use the water on your plants. It's an excellent fertilizer.

Fish Story.

My method of freezing fish preserves that delicate, just-caught flavor, with no freezer burn, *ever*. Fillet fish and rinse in cold water. Place fillets in plastic bag, then pour a mixture of 4 cups cold water and 1 tablespoon table salt into bag. Release any air from bag, seal and freeze.

All Clear.

If your home-brewed iced tea is cloudy, add a little boiling water to the pitcher. The tea will clear immediately!

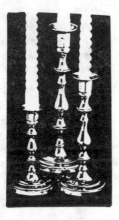

Top Brass.

I love my brass knick-knacks, but detest polishing them. I've found that coating the freshly polished brass with tung oil keeps them clean and shiny for months, allowing me to enjoy my time—and my brass—a lot more! (Note: To remove tung oil when the brass finally begins to look dirty and in need of another cleansing, wipe the brass with paint remover or lacquer thinner, then soak it in very hot, preferably boiling, water. A final wipe with the solvent should remove every last trace of tung oil. But be careful in working with solvent.)

Sweet Shoe.

Does your boy have smelly sneakers? Then make a thin paste of baking soda and water and paint the shoes inside and out with it and let them dry. No more dreadful smell. Repeat every few weeks, as necessary.

I have some plastic water glasses that are stained on the outside. (Not even my dishwasher will remove those stains!) To get these glasses new-looking again, I put a little toothpaste on a sponge and scrub. Toothpaste also removes small scratches from plastic.

To Pop Every Kernel.

If you still pop popcorn the old-fashioned way—with oil and a big pot—this tip should eliminate unpopped corn kernels: Heat oil until sufficiently hot, then add *refrigerated* kernels. You should have really fluffy popcorn!

Sitting Pretty.

Here's an idea for baby when old enough to sit in the bathtub. Place a rectangular plastic laundry basket in the big tub, and pop him into the basket. Water flows in and out, tub toys stay within reach and baby feels secure being able to hold on to the sides of the basket.

Tiny Tycoons.

If your children are reluctant to give up unused possessions, offer to help arrange a garage sale for them, and let them keep the proceeds.

Contact With a Lost Lens.

If you accidentally drop a contact lens on the rug, turn off the lights and pull the shades—make the room as dark as possible—then shine a flashlight over the floor. The lost lens will sparkle when the light hits it.

Cleaner Keys.

When the keys on your typewriter need cleaning, use an old toothbrush and some nail polish remover. They work just as well as commercial typewriter cleaners and are cheaper.

Puppy Love.

This tip is for anyone with a litter of puppies. Place the same number of cloth strips as you have puppies in the bed with their mother. Then send a cloth strip with each puppy to its new home. The puppy will be less apt to cry with its mother's scent nearby.

Take Your Medicine.

Kids and some adults have trouble swallowing nasty-tasting medicine. But sucking on an ice cube just before "numbs" the tastebuds. Medicine becomes almost tasteless.

Moving Right Along.

When you move and need to disassemble anything put together with screws, tape the screws to the item.

Then, at your new location, the screws will be right at hand for reassembling.

Days of the Weak.

To keep track of medical expenditures (office visits, X-rays, prescriptions, etc.), I write them on the December page of our wall calendar. Then when we file our insurance claims, we have an easy-to-find list of what we spent, when and where.

The "Lost" Edge Found.

To find the beginning of that frustrating roll of plastic wrap, take a piece of cellophane tape and touch it to the roll. You will quickly lift up the "lost" edge.

Size It Up.

When preparing clothing for a rummage sale, be sure to mark men's suits (as well as other items) with correct sizes. Having been to many rummage sales, I know that many items—particularly men's suits—could have been sold if they had been marked with the size. Men don't usually accompany their wives to try on items at such sales.

The Brush-off.

To give your dog a fresh smell and a cleaner coat, try sprinkling it with baby powder. Rub the powder into the pet's coat, wait a few minutes, then brush it out.

RECIPES

I do hope you will enjoy these recipes, gathered just for you from great and useful women across America. Even some of my own favorite recipes, gathered from everywhere, are included. As you prepare them—and as you serve them—have fun!

Viola

Shirley Beiler

Betty Box

Judy Coleman

Wanda Cummons

Marlene Evans

Macel P. Falwell

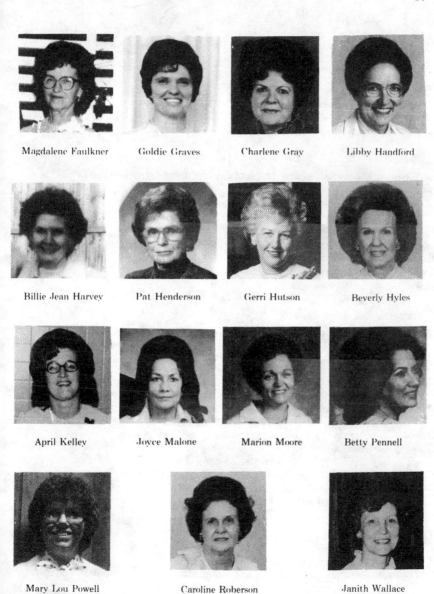

Magdalene Faulkner   Goldie Graves   Charlene Gray   Libby Handford

Billie Jean Harvey   Pat Henderson   Gerri Hutson   Beverly Hyles

April Kelley   Joyce Malone   Marion Moore   Betty Pennell

Mary Lou Powell   Caroline Roberson   Janith Wallace

MALONE MACARONI CHEESE CASSEROLE

1 pkg. Muellers Elbow Macaroni
  (16 oz.)
3 cans Campbells Tomato Soup
1 pkg. Cracker-Barrel Cheese, sharp
1 pkg. Cracker-Barrel Cheese,
  extra sharp

1 pkg. sharp cheddar cheese
½ cup sugar (more if desired to
flavor)
Salt to taste

Directions:

Boil macaroni in sauce pan until quite done (it will bake later).
Add tomato soup, sugar, salt.
Slice cheese (assorted) and layer cheese and macaroni, ending up with layer of cheese (generous with cheese).
Bake at 350⁰ for 20-25 min.

Joyce Malone (Mrs. Tom)
Pontiac, Michigan

MARINATED VEGETABLES

Sauce:

1 can tomato soup
1 cup sugar
¾ cup vinegar
½ cup oil

1 TBS. dry mustard
1 TBS. Worchestershire sauce
½ tsp. salt
¼ tsp. pepper

Raw Vegetables:

½ pound carrots, cleaned and cut in diagonal slices 1/3"
2 green peppers, cut in bite-sized pieces
1 head cauliflower, broken into bite-sized pieces
1 onion, sliced
1 pound fresh mushrooms, cleaned
4-6 stalks of celery, cut in ½" diagonal slices
1 can ripe olives; drain liquid
cherry tomatoes, optional

Mix sugar, dry mustard, salt and pepper. Then gradually add tomato soup (undiluted), stirring constantly. Slowly add oil, vinegar and Worchestershire sauce. Mixture should not contain any lumps. Do not heat.
Put in large glass or plastic jar or bowl.
Prepare vegetables and add to sauce. Marinate overnight in refrigerator. Will keep for several days.

Marlene Evans (Mrs. Wendall)
Hyles-Anderson College

CHEESE BLINTZES

1 loaf fresh sandwich bread
12 oz. cream cheese
¼ cup sugar
1 egg yolk

1 stick oleo, melted
1 cup sugar
1 tsp. cinnamon

Cut crust from entire loaf of bread and roll bread with rolling pin.

Make mixture of cream cheese, ¼ cup sugar and 1 egg yolk. Spread onto each slice of bread. Roll bread up tightly and cut in half. Roll pieces in oleo, and then in mixture of 1 cup sugar and 1 tsp. cinnamon. Place on ungreased cookie sheet and bake at 325° for about 20 min.

Dip in sour cream when serving (or top with).

These are at best when warm, crisp. . .Not too sweet, just right.

Billie Jean Harvey (Mrs. Bill)
Cedar Hill, Texas

CHEESE-SQUASH CASSEROLE

4 cups cooked yellow squash
(fresh or canned)
1 can cream of celery soup
1 sm. jar pimientos (undrained)
1 or 2 green onions, chopped
(tops and bottoms)
Grated carrot (optional)

½ pt. sour cream
½ of 8 oz. pkg. Pepperidge
Farms cornbread stuffing mix
½ stick margarine
8 oz. pkg. shredded mozzarella
cheese

Melt margarine and stir into the stuffing mix; then line bottom of baking dish (approx. 8" x 12¼") with mixture. Mix all other ingredients well and pour over stuffing-lined dish. Bake at 350° approximately 45 min. Remove from oven, sprinkle grated mozzarella on top, and bake about 5 min. or until cheese is melted and bubbly.

Charlene Gray (Mrs. Bob)
Jacksonville, Florida

BILLY GRAHAM'S GRAPEFRUIT SALAD

Dissolve 1½ envelopes of unflavored gelatin in ½ cup cold water. Heat juice from two cans of grapefruit sections in ½ cup water. Add to gelatin, then add one small can crushed pineapple, ¼ cup sugar, grapefruit sections, ½ cup slivered almonds and juice of one lemon. Serves 4 to 6.

CHICKEN SPAGHETTI

1 hen or large chicken
2 medium onions, grated
1 cup celery, chopped
¼ tsp. black pepper
1 can pimientos, chopped
1 can mushroom soup

1 can tomato soup
1 pkg. Italian spaghetti
2 buttons of garlic, grated
¼ tsp. red pepper
½ lb. cheese

Cook chicken in water until tender. Mix other ingredients together and let stand until chicken is done. Let chicken cook enough to take meat off the bones. Cook spaghetti in chicken broth according to directions on package. Stand spaghetti on ends and as it softens push it into broth without breaking it up. Combine all ingredients into a large baking dish and grate cheese over top. Bake in low oven—300⁰—for 45 min. Serve hot.

Pat Henderson (Mrs. A. V.)
Detroit, Michigan

BROCCOLI SOUFFLE

3 pkgs. (10 oz. each) frozen
  broccoli
¼ cup chopped onion
½ cup margarine or butter
2 TBS. flour

1 tsp. salt
½ cup water (may need more)
3 eggs
8 oz. grated cheddar cheese
½ cup bread crumbs

Saute onions in butter. Add flour, salt, water. Melt cheese into mixture. Fold in slightly-beaten eggs. Add broccoli. Cover with crumbs. Bake in 325⁰ oven for 40 to 60 min.

Libby Handford (Mrs. Walter)
Greenville, South Carolina

CHICKEN CASSEROLE

2 cups chicken
2 cups celery
1 cup mayonnaise
2 TBS. lemon juice
½ tsp. salt

2 TBS. grated onion
½ cup slivered almonds
2 cups cheese, grated
2 cups crushed potato chips

Mix all ingredients except cheese and potato chips, which should be sprinkled on top. Bake at 450⁰ for 20 min.

Macel P. Falwell (Mrs. Jerry)
Lynchburg, Virginia

SPICY POT ROAST

3 to 5 lb. beef pot roast
2 TBS. fat
½ cup brown sugar, firmly packed
¼ tsp. salt
½ cup vinegar

¼ cup soy sauce
1 bay leaf crumbled
4 stalks celery
2 medium-sized onions

Brown meat in hot fat in heavy skillet. Mix brown sugar, salt, vinegar, soy sauce and bay leaf. Pour over roast. Add cut-up celery and onion. Cover tightly and cook in 300⁰ oven for two hours or until fork-tender. Remove roast to warm platter. Thicken liquid for gravy if desired. Use 1½ TBS. flour for every cup of broth. This recipe serves 6 to 8 people.

Wanda Cummons (Mrs. Bruce)
Massillon, Ohio

YOGURT

3 cups dry milk
1—13 oz. can evaporated milk
5 cups water
¼ cup sugar

4 TBS. plain yogurt
1 Envelope unflavored gelatin,
    dissolved in 1 cup hot water

Preheat oven to 350⁰. Mix all ingredients thoroughly in a glass bowl and cover with foil. Turn oven off, and place bowl in oven. Leave undisturbed 9½-10 hrs. Refrigerate. Serve plain or with your favorite fruit topping.

Betty Pennell (Mrs. Bill)
Decatur, Georgia

HIBACHI STEAK AND CHICKEN

1 lb. round or sirloin steak
2 chicken breasts or 3 thighs
1 lb. fresh mushrooms or
    large can
1½ lbs. young zucchini

1 can bean sprouts (drained)
1 medium onion
1 TBS. lemon juice
salt, pepper and soy sauce
    to taste

Parboil chicken in a little water; when done, let cool.

Cut steak and chicken into bite-sized pieces. Wash and slice mushrooms. Cut onion in strips. Wash and slice zucchini.

Stir-fry steak till it starts to turn brown. Add onion, let simmer till onions soften. Add chicken, mushrooms, bean sprouts, and zucchini. Stir together. Add lemon juice, salt, pepper and soy sauce to taste. Cover and cook on medium heat till it reaches doneness you desire. Serve on rice if desired. Serves 4 or 5.

Janith Wallace (Mrs. Tom)
Louisville, Kentucky

LAYERED STRAWBERRY SALAD

2—3-oz. boxes strawberry Jello
1½ cups boiling water
2—10-oz. boxes frozen strawberries

1 (#2) can crushed pineapple
2 mashed bananas
½ pint sour cream

Dissolve Jello in boiling water and add frozen strawberries. Stir until strawberries are thawed. When cool and slightly thick, add mashed bananas and crushed pineapple.

Pour half of mixture into pan or bowl and place in refrigerator until solid. For quicker set, place in freezer for a few minutes. Stir sour cream well and spread over the set mixture; then pour the remaining mixture over the top. Let set.

Delicious as either a salad or dessert.

Mary Lou Powell (Mrs. John)
Wadsworth, Ohio

CHICKEN SALAD CASSEROLE

1 cup diced celery
2 TBS. diced onion
1 TBS. margarine
2 cups diced cooked chicken,
  turkey or ham
1 cup cooked rice
1 can water chestnuts, sliced
1 can cream of chicken soup
  (undiluted)

1 cup sour cream
Salt and pepper to taste
1 cup silvered almonds
  optional)
1 cup crushed corn flakes
¼ cup melted margarine

Saute celery and onion in margarine until just clear. Mix with all except last three ingredients and spoon into a greased caserole. Mix the almonds (if used), corn flakes and butter; sprinkle on top. Bake at 350⁰ for 45 min. Will fill a 9 x 13-inch casserole or three small casseroles, each of which will serve 2.

This recipe is good for left-over turkey, chicken, or ham. Freezes well either before baked or reheated afterwards.

Goldie Graves (Mrs. Lonnie)
Durham, North Carolina

LIZ'S BEEF SAUSAGE

8-9 lbs. round beef with
    fat removed
2 TBS. sage
1 tsp. red pepper
2 TBS. freshly ground
    black pepper

1/8 cup salt or diet salt
¼ TBS. marjoram
½ cup cold water

Cut beef into 1-inch squares; mix seasonings well and add water. Add meat to seasoning mixture. Grind meat in food processor or meat grinder. Make into patties. Freeze and store.

The meat can be mixed with bulger wheat and layer bottom of baking dish. Add a layer of cooked rice (1 cup) and top with another layer of meat. Bake 20-30 min.

Mrs. E. J. Daniels
Orlando, Florida

MEAT BALLS A LA SWISS

1 lb. of ground beef
⅓ cup evaporated milk
1 TBS. dried parsley flakes
1 TBS. prepared mustard
1 tsp. salt
¼ tsp. pepper

10½ oz. can cream of chicken soup
½ cup shredded Swiss cheese
⅓ cup evaporated milk
¼ cup water
2 to 3 drops tabasco

Mix first seven ingredients together; shape into sixteen (16) 1½ inch balls. Place in shallow baking pan. Bake in oven at 350⁰ for 20 min. Drain. Mix remaining ingredients together. Pour over meat balls. Bake 10 min. more. Garnish with parsley flakes. Serves four.

Annette Rice (Mrs. Pete)
Murfreesboro, Tennessee

APPLE CRUNCH

Peel and quarter six cooking apples. Put in a Pyrex dish. Cover with following "crumb" mixture:

1 cup sugar
2/3 cup flour

1/3 cup margarine
1 tsp. cinnamon

Bake at 370 degrees.

Magdalene Faulkner (Mrs. J. R.)
Chattanooga, Tennessee

CHICKEN CHOP SUEY

3 TBS. oil
3 medium-sized onions, chopped
4 stalks celery, sliced
1 stewed chicken, skinned
and boned

½ cup sliced mushrooms
2 or 3 cups cooked brown rice
Salt and pepper to taste

Heat oil in large frying pan and saute the onions until tender. Add celery and cook 2 min. longer. Add mushrooms, chicken, and rice. Steam on low heat. Serve with soy or tamari sauce. (May also put grated cheese on top and melt before serving.)

April Kelley (Mrs. Bob)
Murfreesboro, Tennessee

"HEALTH FOOD" SPICE COOKIES

1 cup butter
1 cup honey
½ tsp. cinnamon
½ tsp. cloves
½ tsp. allspice

1 tsp. baking soda
½ tsp. sea salt
2½ cups whole wheat flour
½ cup chopped almonds

Mix together the butter and honey. Add the spices, soda, salt and flour. Blend in almonds. Drop by teaspoonful onto buttered cookie sheet and bake at 350⁰ for about 8 minutes.

Shirley Beiler (Mrs. John)
Kennedyville, Maryland

OUR FAVORITE E'CLAIRS

½ cup Crisco
1/8 tsp. salt
1 cup boiling water

1 cup sifted flour
4 eggs, unbeaten

Add Crisco and salt to boiling water and heat again to boiling. Reduce heat, add flour all at once, stirring until mixture forms ball around spoon, leaving pan clean. Add 1 egg at a time, beating thoroughly after each one. Continue beating till mixture is thick and shiny. Shape on ungreased cookie sheet using about 1 TBS. per e'clair.

Bake at 450⁰ for 20 min., then 350⁰ for 20 additional min. Cool. Slit on side and spoon in vanilla custard. (I often use instant vanilla pudding.) Frost with your favorite chocolate frosting. Makes one dozen.

Beverly Hyles (Mrs. Jack)
Hammond, Indiana

CHOCOLATE SUPREME

CRUST: In 13 x 8 oblong pan:
- 1 cup chopped nuts
- 1½ sticks margarine
- 1½ cups flour

Mix and press in bottom of pan. Bake 350⁰ for 20-25 min. and cool.

1st layer—
- 1½ pkgs. cream cheese (8 oz. & 3 oz.)
- 1½ cups powdered sugar
- 1½ cups Cool Whip

Mix and spread over crust.

2nd layer—
- 1 large instant vanilla pudding mix
- 1 large instant chocolate pudding mix
- 4½ cups milk

Mix and spread on top.

TOPPING: Place Cool Whip on top and shaved chocolate (if desired)

Marion Moore (Mrs. Bob)
Marietta, Georgia

BUTTER-NUT CAKE AND ICING

1 cup Crisco shortening
1 cup milk
2 cups sugar
2¼ cups self-rising flour

4 whole eggs
1 TBS. vanilla-butter-nut
flavoring*

Mix like any cake. Bake in 3 layers.

Icing:

1 stick margarine
1 box powdered sugar
1 8 oz. pkg. cream cheese

1 TBS. flavoring*
1 cup pecans

Beat all together. Add nuts and flavoring last. Will frost 3 layers.

*Flavoring bought by name "Imitation Vanilla-Butter-Nut Flavoring."

Gerri Hutson (Mrs. Curtis)
Murfreesboro, Tennessee

NEIMAN-MARCUS CAKE

1 pkg. yellow cake mix
1 stick butter or margarine
  (melted)
2 eggs

1 box powdered sugar

1 stick butter or margarine
  (melted)
2 eggs
1 (8 oz.) cream cheese,
  softened
fresh strawberry halves

Combine cake mix, first stick of melted butter or margarine and first eggs; mix well; pour into oblong (9 x 13) Pyrex baking dish; combine powdered sugar, second stick of melted butter or margarine and second eggs; mix well; blend in softened cream cheese; mix well; pour over mixture in dish; bake at 300⁰ for 25 minutes; increase heat to 350⁰ and bake for 20 minutes; cool; garnish with fresh strawberry halves at serving time.

Betty Box (Mrs. Clyde)
DeSoto, Texas

PUMPKIN PIE

2 UNBAKED PIE SHELLS

1 large can pumpkin
4 eggs
1 cup brown sugar (packed down)
1 cup white sugar

1 large can evaporated milk
¼ tsp. salt
1 TBS. vanilla
½ tsp. cinnamon
½ tsp. pumpkin pie spice
1 tsp. nutmeg

Beat eggs until light; add sugar, pumpkin and milk and beat until well mixed. Add pumpkin pie spice, cinnamon and vanilla. Pour into pie shells and sprinkle nutmeg on top. Bake 10 min. in preheated 400⁰ oven; then turn oven down to 350⁰ and continue to bake until knife can be inserted, coming out clean—about 45 min.

Top with whipped cream.

Caroline Roberson (Mrs. Lee)
Chattanooga, Tennessee

ORANGE ROLLS

1 envelope yeast
¼ cup very warm water
1 cup sugar
1 tsp. salt
2 eggs

½ cup sour cream
1 stick margarine melted
3½ cups sifted all-purpose flour
2 TBS. grated orange rind

1. Dissolve yeast in the warm water. Beat in ¼ cup sugar, salt, eggs, sour cream and 6 TBS. melted margarine. Gradually add 2 cups flour; beat until smooth. Knead remaining flour into dough.
2. Let rise in bowl about 2 hours till doubled in size.
3. Knead dough on well-floured surface about 15 times.
4. Roll out into a large circle.
5. Combine ¾ cup sugar and orange rind. Brush dough with melted margarine and sprinkle orange-sugar mixture over dough.
6. Roll up "Jelly Roll Fashion" and cut into slices.
7. Place in well-greased pan. Cover and let rise in warm place about an hour.
8. Bake at 350° for 20 min. or until golden brown.
9. Top with glaze.

GLAZE:

¾ cup sugar
½ cup sour cream

2 TBS. orange juice
1 stick margarine

Combine ingredients and boil three min., stirring constantly. Pour over rolls when they are removed from the oven. DELISH!

Judy Coleman (Mrs. Gary)
Garland, Texas

—From Viola

Some of my own favorite recipes, gathered from here and there through the years. . . . . . .

DELICIOUS PARTY PUNCH

1—3 oz. pkg. raspberry Jello
2 cups boiling water
1 small pkg. raspberry Kool-Aid, mixed as directed
1—6 oz. can frozen orange juice, mixed as directed

1—6 oz. can frozen lemonade, mixed as directed
1 large can sweetened pineapple juice
1 cup sugar

Dissolve Jello in boiling water. Combine with remaining ingredients. Chill.

INSTANT RUSSIAN TEA

½ cup instant tea
2 cups Tang
1—3 oz. pkg. imitation-
flavored lemonade mix

¾ cup sugar
½ tsp. cinnamon
½ tsp. allspice
¼ tsp. cloves

Mix and shake. Serve 2 or 3 rounded tsp. per cup, then add boiling water. (Also makes a refreshing cold drink.)

An old standby

CARROT CAKE

Measure into bowl:

1½ cups Wesson oil
4 eggs
2 cups white sugar

Cream well

Sift together 3 cups self-rising flour with 1 tsp. cinnamon. Add this to the above mixture, and mix well.

Add 1 cup of black walnuts,
2 cups grated carrots.

Mix well. Bake in tube pan ½ hour at 250°, 45 min. at 300°. Cool and frost.

FROSTING: (You do not necessarily need frosting, however, if you are calorie-conscious.)

1½ cups of brown sugar
½ cup of white sugar
¼ stick of margarine

1 small can milk
1 tsp. vanilla

Mix together and cook slowly until forms soft ball when dropped in cup of cold water. Remove from heat, cool, beat until thick enough to spread on top and sides of cake.

CARROT LOAF

2 eggs, well beaten
2 cups ground carrots
2 cups dry bread crumbs

2 cups ground meat or salmon
2 cups milk
Salt and pepper to taste

Beat eggs in baking dish. Add other ingredients and mix well. Cover with butter and bake until brown. Very good and easy to make.

DUMP CAKE *(don't let the name fool you!)*

1 can (med. size) crushed pineapple
1 box yellow cake mix (large)
1 cup pecans (broken pieces)
1 can flaked coconut (or fresh)
1½ sticks butter (or margarine)

Distribute ingredients evenly in large, oblong, ungreased cake pan, one on top of the other. Do not mix. Do it this way:

Pour can pineapple with juice into pan. Place coconut on top. Sprinkle on dry cake mix. Slice butter into small patties and arrange over all. Push pecans into mix to center but not to bottom. Bake 45 min. at 350° or until golden brown. Top with cream if desired. You will get raves over this one!

EXTRA SPECIAL FRUIT CAKE

1 lb. Brazil nuts (1¾ cups)
1 lb. walnuts (2¼ cups)
1 lb. dates (3 cups)
1½ cups sugar
1½ cups cake flour
1 tsp. baking powder

pinch of salt
2 med. (3 or 3¾ oz.) bottles
   Maraschino cherries (1 red
   and 1 green)
4 eggs

Do not chop nuts or dates; leave whole. Pour sugar over nuts and dates. Sift together and add cake flour, baking powder and salt. Add red and green cherries and juice. Separate 4 eggs and add beaten egg yolks. Fold in stiffly beaten egg whites last. Bake at 325° for 1 hour and 15 min. Makes 2 loaf-sized cakes.

At any special occasion, my sister-in-law is called on to make the

JEAN WALDEN FRUIT SALAD

3 oranges, sectioned and peeled
3 grapefruit, peeled and membranes pulled off
2 or 3 bananas
1 jar cherries (take out about 12 to top salad) and cut others in two.
2 cans pineapple
1 small can mandarin oranges
Marshmallows
Coconut is optional

Stir it all together, and add the 12 cherries for a beautiful and delicious dish.

My Aunt Ruth kept this cake on hand at all times, made from this recipe. (She did not use a frosting.)

BUTTERMILK CAKE

1 cup Crisco
2 cups sugar
3 eggs—whole—add one at a time
Alternate 3 cups flour with 1 cup buttermilks, and ½ tsp. soda.
Add ½ tsp. salt
2 tsp. vanilla

Pour in large angel food cake pan, cook at 350° for one hour or so. Test with toothpick; if comes up clean, cake is done.

This was a favorite cake with my cousin Ray Walden and his wife Evie:

JELLY CAKE

½ cup Crisco
1 cup sugar
2 eggs
1 tsp. vanilla

1 cup milk
2 cups flour
2 tsp. baking powder

Beat until smooth. Bake in layers that will barely cover the cake pan (should produce 5 layers). While hot, spread with tart jelly (plum) and stack.

FROSTING:

1 stick oleo
½ cup Spry
1 cup granulated sugar

¾ cup warm milk (test like baby's)
1 tsp. vanilla

Beat with electric mixer until light and fluffy (consistency of whipped cream). Spread on top of cake. Add walnut halves if desired.

CEREAL COOKIES *(no cooking)*

Melt together:

½ cup white Karo syrup and ½ cup sugar

Add: 1 cup of chunk style peanut butter and stir until hot.

To the above mixture add 3 cups of "K" or Cornflake cereal.

Pat in 9 x 9-inch pan, but not too hard. Pour 1 pkg. chocolate chips over all. Put in oven for just a few minutes to melt. Spread and let cool before cutting. This is a "quickie" and very, very tasty!

Take my word for it—this is a scrumptious

POPPY SEED CAKE

½ cup butter
1½ cups sugar (see * below)
¾ cup poppy seed that has been soaked 3 hours in 1 cup sweet milk.
2 cups flour
A pinch of salt
2 tsp. baking powder
Whites of 4 eggs beaten stiff and added last.

* (Use ½ cup of sugar with the egg whites out of the sugar above).

Bake in either loaves or in a square pan. Test with toothpick.

FILLING

1½ cups milk
4 egg yolks
¾ cup sugar

Boil 7 min. and thicken with 1½ tsp. cornstarch. Add a layer of filling on top and sides. Sprinkle ½ cup nut meats on top of filling.

CHINESE CHEWS:

¾ cup sifted flour	¼ tsp. salt
1 cup sugar	1 cut chopped walnuts
1 tsp. baking powder	3 well-beaten eggs.

Sift dry ingredients. Stir in remaining ingredients. Pour into greased 10½ x 15½ inch pan. Bake in slow oven 300° for 30 min. Makes 3 dozen.

MILLIONAIRE PIE (Makes 2)

1 can Eagle Brand condensed milk (large)
⅓ cup lemon juice (about 3 lemons)
1 can 15½ oz. crushed pineapple (or 2—8¼ oz. cans)—drained
1—9 oz. carton Cool Whip (4 cups)
½ to 1 cup pecans, chopped
A drop of cake coloring if desired.

Mix, then add Cool Whip. Spoon into 2 graham cracker crusts. Refrigerate several hours. May garnish also with chopped maraschino cherries and coconut. Delightful!

MOCHA TOFFEE BARS

¼ cup butter
1—6 oz. pkg. (1 cup)
   semi-sweet chocolate pieces
2 cups of one-minute
   uncooked quick oatmeal

¾ cup brown sugar
¼ cup light corn syrup
1½ tsp. vanilla
½ tsp. salt

1. Melt butter and chocolate over hot water (double boiler)
2. Combine oatmeal, brown sugar and remaining ingredients. Mix with butter and chocolate.
3. Pack mixture into well-greased pan 11 x 7 x 1½. Bake.
4. When bars are cooled, loosen edges, turn pan over and strike it firmly against counter top so food drops out of pan.

FROST with mixture of square (1 oz.) baking chocolate melted, 1 cup sifted powdered sugar, 2 TBS. hot strong coffee. Sprinkle with ⅓ cup chopped nuts.

Time: 15-18 min., with temperature at 375⁰.

THOUGHTS

Worth Thinking

About!

No matter what one's past may have been, his future is spotless.

Those who wait to repent until the eleventh hour often die at ten thirty.

On his dining room wall Augustine had written these words: "He who speaks evil of an absent man or woman is not welcome at this table."

God always gives His best to those who leave the choice to Him.

—Jim Elliot

When arguing with a fool, always make sure that he is not similarly engaged.

So live that you would not mind giving the family parrot to the village gossip.

—Irish Digest

The wages of sin have never been reduced.

Never put a question mark where God puts a period.

THE CURE FOR CRIME IS NOT THE ELECTRIC CHAIR BUT THE HIGH CHAIR—J. Edgar Hoover.

The measure of one's real character is what he would do if he knew he would never be found out.—Macaulay.

The greatest security against sin is to be shocked at its presence.—Carlyle.

Temptation rarely comes in working hours. It is in our leisure time that we are made or marred.

—W. T. Taylor.

THE CROSS IS THE LAST ARGUMENT OF GOD. —Spurgeon.

The dictionary is the only place where success comes before work.

No physician ever weighed out medicine to his patients with half so much care and exactness as God weighs out to us every trial. Not one grain too much does He ever permit to be put in the scale. —Beecher.

God writes with a pen that never blots, speaks with a tongue that never slips, and acts with a hand that never fails.

Whose Fault?

A young married couple was contacted and invited to the services of the church. This is the record:

THE FIRST CALL:
"We are going to start as soon as the baby gets old enough to come."

ONE YEAR LATER:
"Yes, we promised, but the baby's in that stage where she cries a lot. I don't get anything out of the services, and I know she disturbs other people. When she gets older. . . ."

THREE YEARS LATER:
"I know you think we are awful, but we're not coming to church because Julie doesn't want to go. Why do you think she is different from the other children her age?"

ELEVEN YEARS LATER:
"I'm so glad you called. I want you or some of the elders to see if you can talk to Julie. She is running around with the wrong crowd. Perhaps if the church would provide some kind of entertainment for the young people, she might get interested."

TWO YEARS LATER:
"Yes, Julie is married. They were awfully young, and he is not a member of the church, but we hope it works out."

TEN YEARS LATER:
"Well, Julie has finally married a man who can give her the better things of life. This is her third husband, but she couldn't get along with the others. I had hopes that this one would become a member of the church, but the preacher preached a sermon on marriage and divorce, and he says he will never attend that church again. There must be something wrong with that church or else it would have had a better influence on Julie. Maybe they need to change preachers. I don't know. . . ."

LORD, IS IT I?

—Anon.

You can't take your money with you—but you can send it on ahead.

"My talent is to speak my mind," said a woman to John Wesley. To which Wesley answered, "I am sure, sister, that God wouldn't object if you buried THAT talent."

Watch out for temptation. The more you see of it, the better it looks.

Our children are the only earthly possessions we can take with us to Glory.

Learn to say "no"; it will be of more use to you than to be able to read Latin.—Spurgeon.

When a dove begins to associate with crows, its feathers remain white; but its heart grows black.
—German Proverb

GOD WILL NOT LOOK YOU OVER FOR MEDALS, DEGREES OR DIPLOMAS, BUT FOR SCARS.

No power on earth nor under the earth can make a man do wrong without his own consent.

It is right to be content with what you have, but not with what you are.

All loudspeakers are not necessarily hooked up.

Worry never robs tomorrow of its sorrow; it only saps today of its strength.— A. J. Cronin.

The soul would have no rainbow had the eyes no tears.—Cheney.

God save us all from wives who are angels in the street, saints in the church, and devils at home.
—Spurgeon

Doing nothing is about the most tiresome work in the world because you cannot stop and rest.

A good thing about telling the truth is that you don't have to remember what you say.

Be slow in choosing a friend, slower in changing.— Benjamin Franklin.

I went out to find a friend,
But could not find one there;
I went out to be a friend,
And friends were everywhere!

If you dread growing old, think of the many who never had that privilege. —DeHaan.

It is easier and better to build boys than to repair men.

I am standing on the promises, walking in His footprints, leaning on His everlasting arms, and drinking from the fountain that never runs dry. —Bud Robinson.

Character is what you are in the dark.—D. L. Moody.

If God sends us on stony paths, He will provide us with strong shoes.
—Alexander Maclaren.

IN LIFE YOU STRIVE AND REACH OUT FOR GOLD; IN HEAVEN, YOU WALK ON IT!

Duty makes us do things well, but love makes us do them beautifully.

The basis of friendship is forgetting what you give and remembering what you receive.

Service is love in overalls.

Groanings which cannot be uttered are often prayers which cannot be refused.—Spurgeon.

I will not permit any man to narrow and degrade my soul by making me hate him.—Booker T. Washington.

There are 365 "fear nots" in the Bible—one for every day of the year.

Kindness is the language the dumb can speak and the deaf can hear and understand.

WHAT YOUR CONSCIENCE SAYS IS MORE IMPORTANT THAN WHAT YOUR NEIGHBORS SAY.

Stir the Cabbage, Perry

Many an earnest preacher's wife unwittingly handicaps her husband. About the time he gets in his study, she calls, "Perry, will you stir the cabbage?"

She goes on to explain that she is waxing the floor and just can't quit. So Perry pushes aside his book and lumbers off to the kitchen to stir the cabbage. Later, when he resumes his study, she says to him, "Perry, I just must take this pattern across the street to Mrs. Rudy's. Will you keep the baby?"

So Perry, after a minute trying to hold the baby with one hand and Young's Analytical with the other, decides he has tackled the impossible and forsakes the book. When she returns, Perry decides to try to study in that little room behind the choir, really not a study, but just a corner. He steals quietly away.

But in a few minutes she comes to the window, "Perry, you simply must fix that step or I will break my neck." Perry fixes the step, but Perry comes empty-handed to his pulpit the next Sunday morning. And next year Perry has to move to some other church.

Perry's wife shakes her head in silent wonder, "Why is it that I must go on moving like this?"

Why doesn't someone tell her!

—Selected

(From Friends Evangel)

Lord, when we are wrong, make us willing to change. And when we are right, make us easy to live with.

Rejecting things because they are old-fashioned would rule out the sun and the moon.

Be as careful of the books you read as of the company you keep, for your character will be influenced as much by the one as by the other.

Husband: "In our six years of marriage we haven't been able to agree on anything."
Wife: "It's been seven years, dear."

HE WHO SERVES GOD FOR MONEY WILL SERVE THE DEVIL FOR BETTER WAGES

Sir Roger L'Estrange.

Once upon a time there was a teacher who didn't want an increase in pay; a carpenter who didn't ask for union wages; a man who healed the sick and afflicted whether they had insurance or medicare or whether they didn't. He fed thousands free—AND THEY CRUCIFIED HIM!

One of life's greatest tragedies is to lose God and not miss Him.

Did you hear about the father who fainted when his son asked for the garage keys and came out with the lawnmower?

It is unreasonable to expect a child to listen to your advice and ignore your example.

A diplomatic husband said to his weeping wife, "But dear, how do you expect me to remember your birthday when you never look any older?"

A lie travels around the world while Truth is putting on her boots.
Spurgeon.

Many people spend six days sowing wild oats, then go to church on Sunday and pray for a crop failure.

INSTEAD OF POINTING A CRITICAL FINGER, TRY HOLDING OUT A HELPING HAND.

There's not a right way to do a wrong thing.

People may doubt what you say, but they will always believe what you do.

ONE WHO BUILDS WALLS INSTEAD OF BRIDGES LIVES A LONELY LIFE.

When it is finally settled that a thing is impossible, watch some fellow do it.

God never puts anybody in a place too small to grow in.

The yoke of God does not fit a stiff neck.

WE CANNOT TRULY SAY, "WHOM I SERVE" UNTIL WE HAVE SAID, "WHOSE I AM."

Even though the tongue weighs practically nothing, it's surprising how few persons are able to hold it.

If Christ is the Way, then we waste time traveling any other.

Truth has only to change hands a few times to become fiction.

Sign on the door of a marriage license bureau: "Out to lunch—think it over."

It is better to give others a piece of your heart than a piece of your mind.

The only time to look down on your neighbor is when you are bending over to help her!

WHATEVER YOU DISLIKE IN ANOTHER PERSON, BE SURE TO CORRECT IT IN YOURSELF.

Satan can build a wall around us—and often does—but he can never put a lid on it. So, KEEP LOOKING UP!

RECIPE FOR TROUBLE:
Take one generation of young people. Add one education from which God and the Bible have been removed. Season liberally with much materialism. Mix with a home life where Christ is only a curse word. Allow to harden into adults. —Inner Witness.

Open-minded or empty-headed—it depends on whether you're defining yourself or someone else.

"CONSCIENCE," said an Indian, "is a three-cornered thing in my heart that stands still when I am good, but when I am bad it turns around and the corners hurt a lot. If I keep on doing wrong, the corners wear off, and it does not hurt any more." —Construction Digest.

If the Red Sea is before you, mountains to the left, desert to the right, and the Egyptians are galloping up behind, start praising God, for the situation is ideal. . .for a miracle! —Peter Allard.

Kindness is a language which even the deaf can hear and the blind can read.

Service is the rent we pay for the space we occupy in the world.

Swallowing your pride occasionally will never give you indigestion!

Home is the place where the great are small and the small are great.

Most people are quite happy to suffer in silence, if they are sure everyone knows they are doing it.

A little oil of Christian love will save a lot of friction.

God has given us the privilege of making the choices of life—but He sets the consequences— R. J. Little.

Life is what happens to us while we are making other plans.

The Prodigal Mother

A certain man had a wife and three children. The wife, becoming dissatisfied with housekeeping, and coveting the money being earned by her neighbors, said to her husband, "Husband, secure for me the social security number that falleth to me, and divide unto me a portion of thy trousers. . . ."
With a reluctant heart the husband granted her desire and divided his wardrobe. Not many days later the wife donned slacks and, with tool box under her arm, waved good-bye to the children, and took her journey into a far country and there secured a man's job in a factory. She made big wages, but she associated with the wicked and listened to the vulgar stories that they told. There was a mighty spiritual famine in that land, and she grew lean in her soul. The children, turned loose at the mercy of the neighbors, soon forgot that they had a mother; but the husband remembered the duties of a wife and wished that his wife would return to her home.
The husband dined on cold lunch meat, while the wife tried in vain to fill her stomach with the husks of the cheese crackers that fell from the canteen vendor's machine. And no man gave unto her the respect due unto a lady. One day at rest period as she sat engulfed in cigarette smoke and smutty stories, she came to herself. She said to herself with remorse, "Here I sit, surrounded by vulgarity, and sacrificing the respect due a lady. At home is a deserted husband, while my children roam the streets unrestrained. The money I make seems small compared to peace of mind and soul." In vain she tried to smother her conscience with the thought that she was contributing to the family's economic welfare. So she said to herself, "I will arise and go to my husband and will say unto him, 'Husband, I have sinned against Heaven and neglected my family in a terrible way. I am no more worthy to be called thy wife, nor the mother of thy children. Make me as thy hired housekeeper.' So she gathered her tools together and started home. And when she was yet a long way off, the husband saw her, and clasped her in his arms. And the wife said, "Husband, I am no more worthy to be called thy wife, nor the mother of thy children." But the father said to the children, "Run and bring hither a dress, and the best apron. Put shoes on her feet, and rush to the meat market and get a steak of the fatted calf, and let us have a warm meal once more. For this your mother was lost, and is found." So they rejoiced and made merry.

—Maranatha

GREAT MINDS DISCUSS IDEAS. AVERAGE MINDS DISCUSS EVENTS. LITTLE MINDS DISCUSS PEOPLE.

Think on your own faults the first part of the night—when you are awake, and the faults of others the latter part of the night—when you are asleep.

The most difficult school is the school of hard knocks—from which one never graduates.

IF YOU WANT ROSES IN NOVEMBER, YOU WILL HAVE TO PUT THEM OUT IN THE SPRINGTIME OF LIFE.

—Henry A. Porter.

A Woman's Hands

What kind of hands do you have? Are they long and slender? Or are they short and plump? Are they rough and red? Or are they smooth and soft? Maybe they are strong and steady or maybe they are weak and shaky. I don't know which of these things are true of you; but if you are a mother, I think I can safely say your hands are *full!*

When you husband was courting you, his first show of affection probably was to hold your hand. It was your hands, more than anything else, that gave your baby assurance of your love and protection.

My mother knows whether or not her pie crust will be good by the feel of the dough in her hands. And what woman would buy a piece of material that she had not first run her hand carefully over?

The Bible has a lot to say about hands. In fact, long before the FBI knew it, God told us in Job 37:7 that a man could be traced through his fingerprints. And as far as a woman's hands—if you'll check the verses concerning the "virtuous woman" in Proverbs 31, you'll find the words *"her hands"* used seven times. They tell us that she worked willingly with her hands, planting a vineyard, making cloth, caring for the poor and her houshold in general.

If God feels that the feet of a preacher are beautiful because they are used to spread the news of the Gospel, then surely He must think busy, helping hands the loveliest part of a woman. Remember the little song the children sing: "Oh, be careful little hands what you do. Oh, be careful little hands what you do. There's a Father up above looking down in tender love, so be careful little hands what you do."

Say, what kind of hands do you have???

—Mrs. Richard Sandlin, Pensacola, Florida

Why do families use money they haven't earned, to buy things they don't need, to impress people they don't like!

THERE ARE NO TRAFFIC JAMS ON THE STRAIGHT-AND-NARROW WAY.

The Devil is not afraid of the Bible that has dust on it.

Criminals are home-grown.

—J. Edgar Hoover.

Keep your words sweet—you may have to eat them.

Some folks occasionally say, "I'd die for Jesus!" He doesn't ask you to die for Him—He asks you to live for Him, and that's more difficult to do.

Babies: angels whose wings grow shorter as their legs grow longer.

He who tells the faults of others to you will tell yours to the other fellow at his first opportunity.

If it were not for the hot water the teakettle would not sing.

The brook would lose its song if you took the rocks away.

Money is an article which may be used as a universal passport to everywhere except Heaven, and as a universal provider of everything except happiness.

In spite of inflation, the wages of sin remain unchanged.

ONE CANNOT SUCCESSFULLY WALK WITH THE LORD WHILE RUNNING WITH THE WORLD.

A lady walked into a supermarket in a desperate attempt to get supper ready quick and asked one of the grocery clerks, "Do you have anything quicker than instant?"

The church is filled with willing people—some willing to work and others willing to let them.

What I kept, I lost,
What I spent, I had,
What I gave, I have.

— **Persian Proverb.**

The minister asked a group of children in a Sunday school class, "Why do you love God?" He got a variety of answers, but the one he liked best was from a boy who said, "I don't know, sir. I guess it just runs in our family."

A day of worry is more exhausting than a week of work.

A WOMAN'S FONDEST WISH IS TO BE WEIGHED AND FOUND WANTING!

Eternity never grows older.

By yielding to temptation one may lose in a moment what it took him a lifetime to gain.

Faith is telling a mountain to move and being shocked only if it doesn't.

Mother, having finally tucked a small boy into bed after an unusually trying day: "Well, I've worked today from son-up to son-down!"

When a child reaches age 14, he has already seen 18,000 human beings killed on television.

—*Christian Teacher.*

A mother asked a psychologist, "When shall I start training my child?" "How old is he?" she was asked. "Five." The psychologist said, "Madam, hurry home! You've already lost five years!"

I Am a Mother's Prayer

I want to introduce you to a mother's prayer, one of the mightiest influences that God ever released through human channels; and yet you may not be able to see our guest, nor hear the actual voice. I shall read the biography of a mother's prayer.

"I am a mother's prayer. I am sometimes clothed in beautiful language that has been stitched together with the needles of love in the quiet chambers of the heart, and sometimes I am arrayed only in the halting phrases interrupted by tears which have been torn like living roots from the deep soil of human emotion. I am a frequent watcher of the night. I have often seen the dawn break over the hills and flood the valleys with light, and the dew of the gardens has been shaken from my eyes as I waited and cried at the gates of God.

"I am a mother's prayer: there is no language I cannot speak; and no barrier of race or color causes my feet to stumble. I am born before the child is born, and ere the day of deliverance comes, I have often stood at the altars of the Lord with the gift of an unborn life in my hands, blending my joyful and tearful voice with the prayers and tears of the father. I have rushed ahead of the nurse through the corridors of the hospital praying that the babe would be perfect, and I have sat dumb and mute in the presence of delight over a tiny bit of humanity, so overwhelmed I have been able to do nothing but strike my fingers on the harps of gratitude and say, "Well, thank the Lord!"

"I am a mother's prayer: I have watched over the cradle; I have sustained a whole household while we waited for a doctor to come. I have mixed medicine and held up a thermometer when the fever read: 104°. I have sighed with relief over the sweat in the little one's curls because the crisis was past. I have stood by a graveside and picked a few flowers to take home like old memories, and cast my arms around the promises of God to just hang on and wait until I could feel underneath me in the everlasting arms.

"I am a mother's prayer: I have walked and knelt in every room of the house: I have fondled the old Book, sat quietly at the kitchen table, and been hurled around the world to follow a boy who went to war. I have sought through hospitals and army camps and battlefields. I have dogged the steps of sons and daughters in college and university, in the big city looking for a job. I have been in strange places, for I have even gone down into honky-tonks and dens of sin, into night clubs and saloons and back alleys and along dark streets. I have ridden in automobiles and planes and ships seeking and sheltering and guiding and reminding and tugging and pulling toward home and Heaven.

"I am a mother's prayer: I have filled pantries with provision when the earthly provided was gone. I have sung songs in the night when there was nothing to sing about but the faithfulness of God. I have been pressed so close to the promises of the Word that the imprint of their truth is fragrant about me. I have lingered on the lips of the dying like a trembling melody echoed from Heaven.

"I am a mother's prayer: I am not unanswered, although mother may be gone, although the home may be dissolved into dust, although the little marker in the graveyard grows dim. I am still here: and as long as God is God, and truth is truth, and the promises of God are 'yea and amen,' I will continue to woo and win and strive and plead with boys and girls whose mothers are in Glory, but whose ambassador I have been appointed by the King Emmanuel. I am a mother's prayer. . . . ."

(From a tract published by the Osterhus Publishing House, 4500 W. Broadway, Minneapolis, Minn., USA.)

What Is a Grandmother?
(Written by a third grader)

A grandmother is a lady who has no children of her own, so she likes other people's girls and boys. A grandfather is a man grandmother. He goes for walks with the boys and they talk about fishing and tractors and like that. Grandmothers don't have anything to do but be there.

They're old, so they shouldn't play hard or run. It is enough if they drive you to the market where the pretend horse is and have lots of dinner ready, or if they take you for walks they should slow down past things like pretty leaves or caterpillars. They should never say "hurry up."

Usually they are fat, but not too fat to tie kid's shoes. They wear glasses and funny underwear, and they can take their teeth and gums off.

It is better if they don't typewrite or play cards except with us. They don't have to be smart, only answer questions like "why dogs hate cats and how come God isn't married." They don't talk baby-talk like visitors do because it is hard to understand.

When they read to us, they don't skip pages or mind if it is the same story again. Everybody should have one, especially if you don't have television, because grandmas are the only grownups who have got time.

NATURE COULDN'T MAKE US PERFECT, SO SHE DID THE NEXT BEST THING—SHE MADE US BLIND TO OUR FAULTS.

A woman who creates and sustains a home, and under whose hands children grow up to be strong and pure men and women, is a creator second only to God.

I can complain because rose bushes have thorns or rejoice because thorn bushes have roses. It's all in how you look at it.

Everyone can give pleasure in some way. One person may do it by coming into a room, another by going out.

Together Still

Let me hold your hand as we go downhill,
We've shared our strength and we share it still.
It hasn't been easy to make the climb,
But the way was eased by your hand in mine.

Like the lake, our life has had ripples, too,
Ill-health, and worries, and payment due,
With happy pauses along the way,
A graduation, a raise in pay.

At the foot of the slope, we will stop and rest,
Look back, if you wish; we've been truly blessed,
We've been spared the grief of being torn apart
By death, or divorce, or a broken heart.

The view ahead is one of the best,
Just a little bit farther, and then we can rest.
We move more slowly, but together still,
Let me hold your hand as
                    we go
                        downhill. . . .

Poem and photo by Peggy Cameron King. —Mississippi Baptist

An Advantage List for Children

To the Editor:

I want my children to have all the advantages I can give them.

Such as having to earn their own allowance by running errands, cutting lawns, learning to sew and to keep their own room straight.

Such as being proud to be clean and decent.

Such as standing up and standing proud when our country's flag goes by.

Such as being kind to all younger children and polite to elder friends and relatives, addressing them as "sir" and "ma'am."

Such as having to earn their own way in the world and knowing they have to prepare for it by hard work, hard study and sacrificing some of the pleasure and ease that their friends may get from too-indulgent parents.

Such as giving their respect to policemen, letting them know they're behind them one hundred per cent.

Such as being a student, unselfish, honest, forgiving and conscious at all times respecting their teacher as a parent.

These are the advantages I want my children to have, because these are the things which will make them self-respecting, self-reliant and successful, with the opportunity to overcome obstacles through prejudices of men. Remembering God is no respector of persons, neither shall they.

Mrs. Carrie Bartlet

Gallatin, Tennessee

(From *Nashville Tennessean*)

How Much Does a Prayer Weigh?

How much does a prayer weigh? There is a story of a man who tried to weigh one. He owned a little grocery store. It was the week before Christmas, shortly after World War I.

A tired-looking woman came into the store and asked for enough food to make a Christmas dinner for the children. The grocer asked her how much she could spend.

"My husband did not come back; he was killed in the War. And I have nothing to offer but a little prayer," she answered.

The storekeeper was not very sentimental or religious, so he said, half mockingly, "Write it on paper, and I'll weigh it."

To his surprise, the woman took a piece of paper from the pocket of her dress and handed it to the man, saying, "I wrote it during the night while watching over my sick baby."

The grocer took the piece of paper before he could recover from his surprise and, because other customers were watching and had heard his remarks, he placed the unread prayer on the weight side of his old-fashioned scales. Then he began to pile food on the other side; but to his amazement, the scale would not go down. In his embarrassment, he continued to put food on the scale, but still the scale refused to go down.

He became angry and flustered and finally said, "Well, that's all the scale will hold. Here's a bag; you will have to put it in yourself. I'm busy."

With trembling hands the woman filled the bag, and through moist eyes expressed her gratitude and departed.

Now that the store was empty of customers, the grocer examined the scales. Yes, they were broken, and they had become broken just in time for God to answer the prayer of the woman.

But as the years passed, the grocer often wondered about the incident. Why did the woman come at just the right time? Why had she already written the prayer in such a way as to confuse the grocer so that he did not examine the scales?

The grocer is an old man now, but the weight of the paper still lingers with him. He never saw the woman again, nor had he seen her before that date. Yet he remembered her more than any of his customers.

And he treasures the slip of paper upon which the woman's prayer had been written—simple words, but from a heart of faith, "Please, Lord, give us this day our daily bread."

—Selected

A THANKFUL OLD LADY:

As an elderly lady with arthritis sat by her window watching the traffic go by, she said, "I don't know what I'd do without it."

Later on she was moved to a room in the rear where she could no longer see the traffic from her window. She commented, "I like this better. The sweetest children play in the back yard next door."

At last she was moved to the slums of the city. To a friend she said, "Come and see my beautiful view—my beautiful view of the sky!"

The only exercise some people get is pushing their luck, running down their friends, sidestepping responsibility, and jumping to conclusions.

If you can't do what you like, suppose you try liking what you do—and see what happens.

THINK IT OVER

Never be afraid to admit that you are wrong; for it is equal to saying that you are wiser today than you were yesterday.

When God puts a tear in your eye, it's because He wants to put a rainbow in your heart!